Handmade Jewelry

SIMPLE STEPS TO CREATING WEARABLE ART

CAROL GRAPE

NORTH LIGHT BOOKS

CINCINNATI, OHIO

A B O U T   T H E   A U T H O R

Photo Credit: Michael D'Innocente

Carol Grape is a sculptor currently living in Northern Kentucky. She received her BFA (1978) in sculpture from the Maine College of Art (formerly the Portland School of Art) and her MFA (1982) in sculpture from Kent State University in Ohio. She lived in New York City from 1983 to 1989. In New York she worked as an apartment painter, interior construction assistant, an artists' assistant to Miriam Schapiro, Dennis Oppenheim and Frank Gardner, the assistant to the president of the Women's Caucus for Art, and a gallery assistant at Steinbaum Kraus Gallery (formerly Steinbaum Gallery).

Since living in Kentucky she's had her first one-person show and has worked at the Art Academy of Cincinnati as an arts administrator and instructor. She is also the gallery director at Thomas More College in Kentucky where she teaches part-time. She has started a jewelry business and a new service business for artists called Art Smart.

METRIC CONVERSION CHART

To Convert	To	Multiply by
Inches	Centimeters	2.54
Centimeters	Inches	0.4

Handmade Jewelry: Simple Steps to Creating Wearable Art. Copyright © 1996 by Carol Grape. Printed and bound in Hong Kong. All rights reserved. No part of this book may be reproduced in any form or by any electronic or mechanical means including information storage and retrieval systems without permission in writing from the publisher, except by a reviewer, who may quote brief passages in a review. Published by North Light Books, an imprint of F&W Publications, Inc., 1507 Dana Avenue, Cincinnati, Ohio 45207. (800) 289-0963. First edition.

Other fine North Light Books are available from your local bookstore or direct from the publisher.

00 99 98 97 96   5 4 3 2 1

Library of Congress Cataloging-in-Publication Data

Grape, Carol
    Handmade jewelry : simple steps to creating wearable art / Carol Grape
        p.   cm.
    Includes index.
    ISBN 0-89134-660-0(alk. paper)
    1. Jewelry making. 2 Wearable art. I. Title.
TT212.G74   1996
745.594'2—dc20   95-51402
                                                                                  CIP

Edited by Greg Albert and Julie Wesling Whaley
Designed by Brian Roeth
Cover photography by Pamela Monfort Braun/Bronze Photography

North Light Books are available for sales promotions, premiums and fund-raising use. Special editions or book excerpts can also be created to specification. For details contact: Special Sales Manager, F&W Publications, 1507 Dana Avenue, Cincinnati, Ohio 45207.

ACKNOWLEDGMENTS

First, I want to thank Jeanne Schmidt at the Art Academy of Cincinnati for suggesting me when Greg Albert, senior editor at North Light Books, called looking for an artist who made funky jewelry. And I want to thank Greg for inviting me to write this, my first book, and for all the help and encouragement. It has been a plesure working with him.

A special thanks to Julie Whaley, the content editor, Katie Carroll, the production editor, and Brian Roeth, the designer of this book, who worked to make it clear, visually exciting and usable.

I want to thank all the artists who took the time to send me slides of their work for consideration. I saw some wonderful work and I wish I could have included more.

I want to thank my great long distance friends, Nancy McKinnon in New England and Sandi Knell Tamny in northeast Ohio, for their support and encouragement. Over the years I've learned a great deal about jewelry from Nancy by watching her work as a metalsmith. Sandi, a sculptor, has been a wonderful client and has encouraged many others to purchase my polymer clay jewelry.

I would like to thank my sisters, Cathy Grape and Caroline Mitchell, and my brother-in-law, Chris Mitchell, for all their love and support over the years. They have also been great clients.

I would expressly like to thank my husband, Mike D'Innocente, for all his love, support and understanding, especially as I kept the photo equipment set up in the family room for months on end. I even wrangled him into taking some shots for this book.

And last, but not least, I'd like to thank my folks, Don and Nancy Grape, for fully supporting my choice to become an artist and especially a sculptor. It makes life so much easier.

TABLE OF CONTENTS

Introduction 7

Chapter One

TOOLS AND TECHNIQUES.... 8

Tools of the Trade . . . 8

Jewelry Findings . . . 9

Gluing Pin Backs on With Hot Glue . . . 10

Opening and Closing Jump Rings . . . 10

Forming an Eye Loop on a Headpin . . . 11

Finishing a Tiger Tail With a Crimp Bead . . . 11

Placing a Crimp on the End of a Cord . . . 12

Using a Dremel Moto Tool to Drill Holes . . . 12

Cutting With a Jeweler's Saw . . . 13

Using Sterling Wire to Hold Findings in Place . . . 13

Chapter Two

FOUND OBJECTS AND HARDWARE ... 15

PROJECT ONE
Stacked Button Pins . . . 16

PROJECT TWO
Squiggly Button Barrettes . . . 18

PROJECT THREE
Elastic Button Bracelet . . . 20

PROJECT FOUR
Electrically Connected Earrings . . . 22

PROJECT FIVE
Resistor Earrings . . . 24

PROJECT SIX
Hardware Charm Necklace . . . 26

PROJECT SEVEN
Fancy Resistor & Bead Necklace . . . 28

PROJECT EIGHT
Cable Tie Earrings & Pin . . . 30

PROJECT NINE
Fabric Covered Gasket Pin & Earrings . . . 32

PROJECT TEN
Brass Gasket Earrings . . . 34

PROJECT ELEVEN
Folded Window Screen Earrings & Pin . . . 36

PROJECT TWELVE
Faucet Strainer Earrings & Necklace . . . 38

PROJECT THIRTEEN
Anodized Aluminum Pin & Earrings . . . 40

Gallery of Found Objects & Hardware Jewelry . . . 42

Chapter Three

PAPER, FIBER AND WOOD...45

PROJECT FOURTEEN
Collage Paper Pins . . . 46

PROJECT FIFTEEN
Folded Gift Paper Pin
& Earrings . . . 48

PROJECT SIXTEEN
Sponge Painted Paper Hearts . . . 50

PROJECT SEVENTEEN
Layered Tissue Paper Earrings & Pin . . . 52

PROJECT EIGHTEEN
Fabric Collage Pins . . . 54

PROJECT NINETEEN
Rolled Ribbon Earrings & Pin . . . 56

PROJECT TWENTY
Embellished Pillow Pins . . . 58

PROJECT TWENTY-ONE
Poly-fil Bead Necklace & Earrings . . . 60

PROJECT TWENTY-TWO
Woodsie Earrings & Pin . . . 62

PROJECT TWENTY-THREE
Constructed Wood Pin . . . 64

PROJECT TWENTY-FOUR
Dyed, Turned Wood
Earrings & Pin . . . 66

PROJECT TWENTY-FIVE
Wood Hand Pin
& Earrings . . . 68
Gallery of Paper, Fiber
& Wood Jewelry . . . 70

Chapter Four

PLASTIC AND RUBBER...73

PROJECT TWENTY-SIX
Plastic Confetti Earrings & Pin . . . 74

PROJECT TWENTY-SEVEN
Plastic Grid Necklace and Earrings . . . 76

PROJECT TWENTY-EIGHT
Cut Out Plastic Laminate Earrings
& Pin . . . 78

PROJECT TWENTY-NINE
Recycled Plastic Disks With
Dangling Beads . . . 80

PROJECT THIRTY
Friendly Plastic Pins & Earrings . . . 82

PROJECT THIRTY-ONE
Plastic Tube Necklace & Bracelet
With Seed Beads . . . 86

PROJECT THIRTY-TWO
Fun Foam Earrings & Pin . . . 88

PROJECT THIRTY-THREE
Rubber O-Ring Gasket Bracelet . . . 90

PROJECT THIRTY-FOUR
Stacked Colorful Rubber Tubing Necklace
& Earrings . . . 92

PROJECT THIRTY-FIVE
Black Sheet Rubber Necklace
& Earrings . . . 94
Gallery of Plastic & Rubber Jewelry . . . 96

Chapter Five

POLYMER CLAYS . . . 99

How to Handle Polymer Clay . . . 100

PROJECT THIRTY-SIX
> FIMO Earrings, Pin, Necklace &
> Barrette . . . 101

PROJECT THIRTY-SEVEN
> Sculpey III Striped Spiral
> Buttons . . . 104

PROJECT THIRTY-EIGHT
> Sculpey III Herringbone Pattern
> Pins & Coiled Earrings . . . 106

PROJECT THIRTY-NINE
> Fun FIMO Face Pins & Earrings . . . 108

PROJECT FORTY
> Marbled Bead Necklace, Earrings
> & Bracelet . . . 110

PROJECT FORTY-ONE
> Spiral Cane Made of FIMO
> Leftovers . . . 112

PROJECT FORTY-TWO
> Polka-Dot FIMO Cane . . . 114

PROJECT FORTY-THREE
> Black & White FIMO Face Cane . . . 117

Gallery of Polymer Clay Jewelry . . . 120

Resources . . . 122

Index . . . 123

INTRODUCTION

Welcome to the wonderful world of jewelry making! The projects in this book are fun and easy and don't require any previous jewelry-making skills. You will learn some simple techniques that will enhance your pieces and give them a very professional look.

The materials used in this book are quite commonplace, found in many small retail craft, hardware and bead stores. Whether you are a first-time or advanced crafter, these projects offer new and creative ways to use non-traditional jewelry materials to make exciting pieces that will enhance any ensemble. This will teach you the skills to develop your own projects that express your unique ideas.

Chapters two through four are an exploration of a variety of materials used in unusual ways as jewelry. It was a challenge and a great deal of fun coming up with these projects. Some I had made before, such as the Squiggly Button Barrettes, the Sponge-Painted Paper Hearts and the Woodsie Earrings. It was exciting to look at things in my house and the hardware store and visualize them as jewelry. I also spent much time wandering through craft supply stores looking at new materials wondering how I could do something that was different and interesting.

A few projects failed, but I was glad to have so many successes. My hope is that after you have made the projects that excite you, you will discover new and interesting ways to use these and other materials.

The final chapter is about polymer clay—a material I've worked with for quite some time. It is very seductive once you get started. The projects in this book are pretty easy, yet time-consuming. Once you have done these, you will easily be able to design and build your own patterns, canes and projects.

To inspire you further, there is a gallery of artists' work at the end of each chapter to show how some other professional artists have used similar materials.

Most importantly, the projects in this book are fun and easy to complete. The techniques provide a professional look for pieces that you'll be proud to wear, sell or give to your family or friends. I wish you lots of fun and success. Enjoy!

Chapter One

TOOLS AND TECHNIQUES

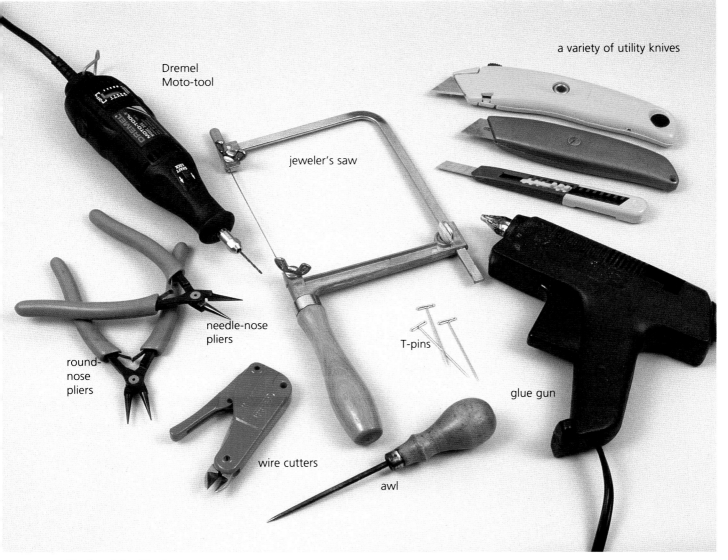

Tools of the Trade.

The techniques described in this section will be helpful for most of the projects. I recommend taking the time to read this section before you plunge into the projects. Most of these techniques describe how to use "jewelry findings." Jewelry findings are the pieces of hardware used to make jewelry, such as ear wires, clasps and pin backs. If you are unfamiliar with some of these techniques, especially cutting with the jeweler's saw, you may wish to practice on some scrap materials.

Not all the tools or all of the findings are used in each project. So, if you are just starting, pick a project first and then buy the tools and materials required. This will help you build equipment and supplies within your budget.

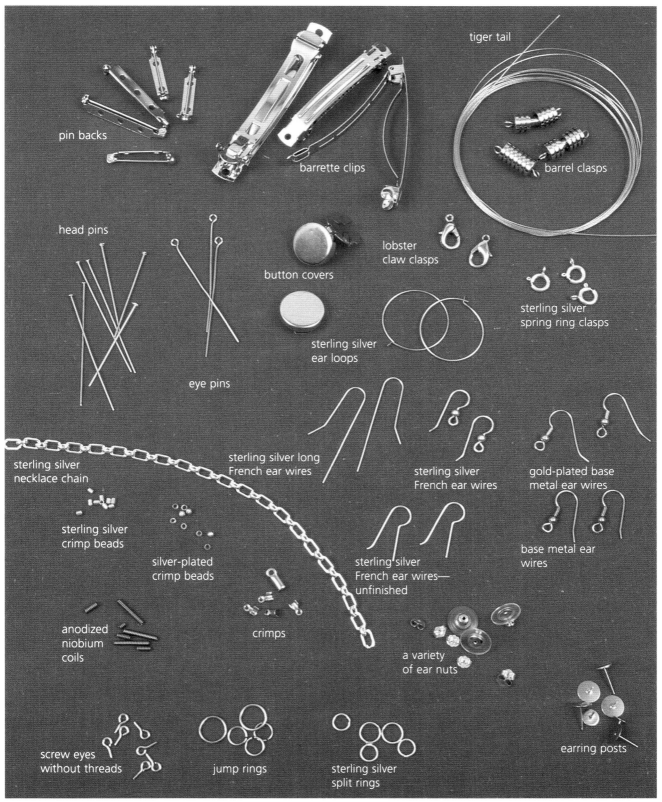

pin backs

barrette clips

tiger tail

barrel clasps

head pins

button covers

lobster claw clasps

sterling silver spring ring clasps

eye pins

sterling silver ear loops

sterling silver necklace chain

sterling silver long French ear wires

sterling silver French ear wires

gold-plated base metal ear wires

sterling silver crimp beads

silver-plated crimp beads

crimps

sterling silver French ear wires— unfinished

base metal ear wires

anodized niobium coils

a variety of ear nuts

screw eyes without threads

jump rings

sterling silver split rings

earring posts

Jewelry Findings.

Gluing Pin Backs on With Hot Glue.

In the location where you want to place the pin back, run a bead of hot glue approximately ⅛" wide and slightly shorter than the length of the pin back. Push the pin into the glue so the glue oozes up into the holes of the pin back and forms a secure bond. It will cool and set up within a few minutes. Remember, this glue is very hot unless you are using a low-melt glue gun. When using cyanoacrylate glue, it is easier to put the glue directly on the pin back and then put it in place. To keep the pin from falling off your clothing, make sure the opening of the pin back is facing the bottom of the piece of jewelry.

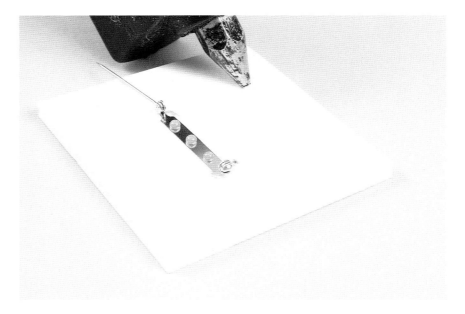

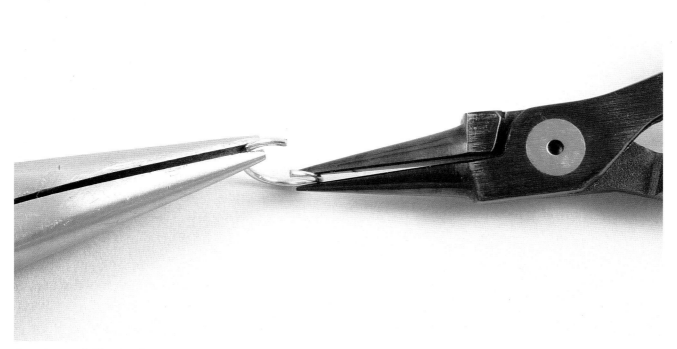

Opening and Closing Jump Rings.

Using two pairs of needle-nose pliers, pry the jump ring open by pushing one pair forward (away from you) and pulling one pair toward you. This keeps the circle of the jump ring from distorting and it allows you to close it as tightly as possible. If you only have one pair of needle-nose pliers, you can usually use your fingers to push one side.

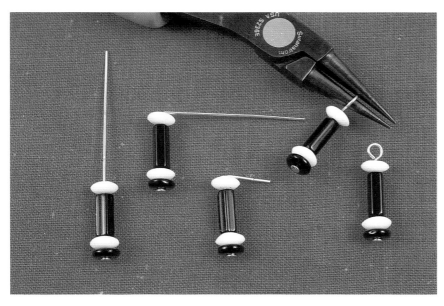

Forming an Eye Loop on a Head Pin.
Once you have stacked your beads on the head pin, fold the pin over 90°, tight to the last bead. Trim the head pin so the folded piece is approximately ⅜″ long. Using round-nose pliers, grasp the end of the pin and roll it back toward the fold forming a circle. To tighten the circle, or to open it to attach it to something else, use the same method as opening and closing a jump ring. I used 2″-long head pins for all of these projects even though I trimmed a lot off some of them. It is cheaper to buy in bulk, and, for me, the 2″ seems to be the best length.

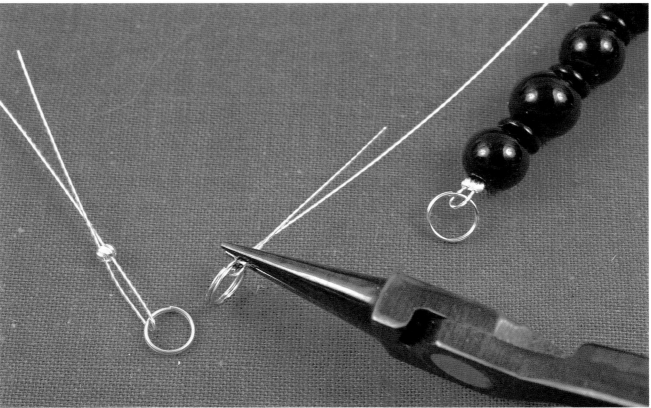

Finishing Tiger Tail With Crimp Beads.
Put a crimp bead on the tiger tail, then loop the tiger tail through a split ring and back through the crimp bead. Slide the crimp bead down to within ⅛″ of the ring and put a drop of cyanoacrylate glue inside the bead. Press this flat with needle-nose pliers. Slide the beads down so the loose end of the tiger tail is inside the beads. Do the same on the other end of the tiger tail but draw the end of the tiger tail through a few beads and pull it with needle-nose pliers in order to get it fairly tight. There should be a bit of space between the glass beads and the crimp bead to allow the necklace or bracelet to flex and lay properly. Once the crimp bead is locked in, trim the tiger tail and tuck it into a bead.

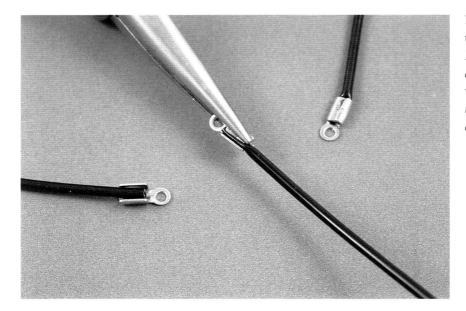

Placing a Crimp on the End of a Cord.

Lay the cord in the channel of the crimp. Fold one side of the crimp over with needle-nose pliers and crimp tight. Fold the second side over and crimp tight and flat.

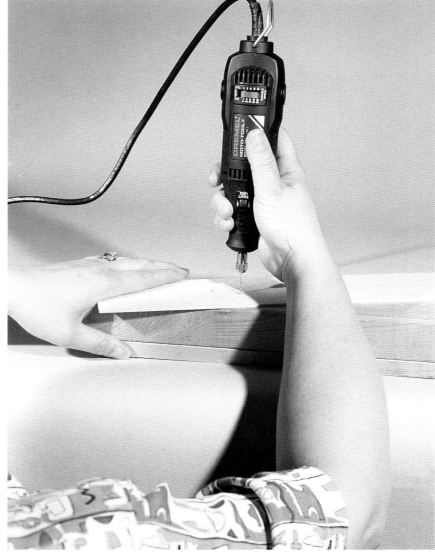

Using a Dremel Moto-tool to Drill Holes.

The same size drill bit can probably be used for every project in this book in which drilling is required. The size I use is ¹⁄₃₂″. Make sure to keep the drill bit perpendicular to the surface you are drilling into. It is a good idea to use a piece of wood under all projects to protect the surface you are drilling on and keep the back side of the hole from splaying out and splintering. Let the drill do the work, there is no need to bear down.

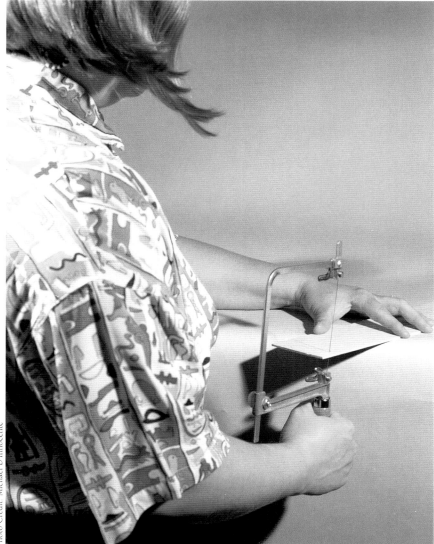

Cutting With a Jeweler's Saw.

Place the blade in the saw so the teeth are pointing down toward the handle. Always keep the blade perpendicular to the cutting surface. Keep your arm at your side and in one location, and move the saw up and down from the elbow. When cutting curves or changing direction, turn the piece you are cutting and keep the saw in the same place. To help the blade move more smoothly through what you are cutting, run it through a piece of beeswax first. These blades break very easily and you will go through a few fairly quickly before you get the hang of it. Because a jeweler's saw is usually adjustable, a broken blade can still be used if it is still large enough.

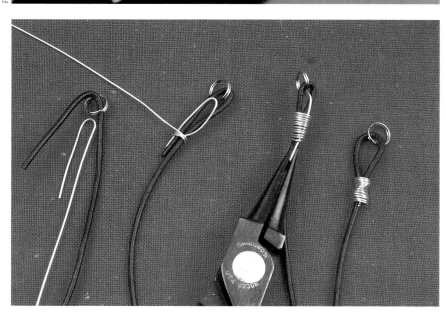

Using Sterling Wire to Hold Findings in Place.

Cut a 6"-long piece of 24-gauge sterling silver wire. Loop the cord through the finding and fold at ¾". Fold the end of the wire at ¾" and lay it on top of the folded cord. Begin wrapping at the end—away from the fold— leaving approximately ⅛" of the wire and cord exposed. Continue wrapping, keeping the wire as tight as possible. Use needle-nose pliers to fold the end into place and pull the end of the wire so the loop tucks in and tightens the wrapping. Trim the excess wire and cord.

Chapter Two

FOUND OBJECTS AND HARDWARE

Found objects are just that—wonderful objects found in your home or out in the world. Artists have used these in sculpture and painting since the early part of this century. It has also become very popular in jewelry making. Some found objects have been cast into gold and silver, others have been used directly. Sometimes found objects are manipulated and sometimes they're combined with other objects to create exciting results.

Finding objects at flea markets, yard sales and hardware stores is great fun. Just imagining that you can turn an ordinary object into a unique piece of jewelry can be quite a challenge. Once you have had a chance to build some of the projects in this section you will definitely approach the hardware store with a new eye. And you will find yourself searching for small unique objects at those yard sales and flea markets. But, before you head to these places looking for materials for these projects, check your junk drawers, sewing closet, attic and garage. You just may find most of what you need right at home.

Stacked Button Pins

STEP ONE Choose 3 to 4 buttons that work well together. Consider shape, color and size.

STEP TWO If you have fairly flat buttons you can glue them together with cyanoacrylate glue. If you have hollow-back buttons, hot glue is your best choice. If you are stacking buttons without shanks (projections on the backs of solid buttons), centered on top of each other, you can usually tie them together with button thread.

STEP THREE Glue on the pin back.

MATERIALS

Decorative buttons
1"-1½" pin backs
Cyanoacrylate glue
Hot glue

TOOLS

Glue gun

OPTIONAL

Sewing needle and button thread

▶ *A variety of Stacked Button Pins using old decorative buttons found at flea markets and yard sales.*

A selection of interesting buttons.

Gluing buttons together.

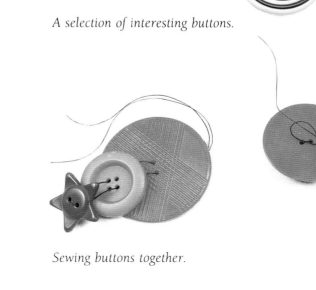

Sewing buttons together.

Squiggly Button Barrettes

STEP ONE Select 3 to 4 buttons that, when overlapped, will cover the barrette clips you have chosen. Shank buttons work well on top but not underneath.

STEP TWO Cut 8″ lengths of phone wire—one for each button.

STEP THREE Remove the spring arch pieces from the back of the barrette clips.

STEP FOUR Tie the buttons on the barrette clips with the phone wires. Draw the wire from under the clips through the holes in the buttons and twist.

STEP FIVE Wrap the ends of the wire around the awl or rod to create a spring-shaped coil.

STEP SIX Use hot glue to keep the buttons in place. Place glue under the buttons and a dab on the wire on the underside of the clips.

STEP SEVEN Reinsert the spring arch after the glue sets up.

MATERIALS
A variety of decorative buttons
Barrette clips
Colored phone wire
Hot glue
TOOLS
Glue gun
Awl or ⅛″- to ¼″-diameter rod

▶ *Squiggly Button Barrettes using colored phone wire as fasteners and as decoration.*

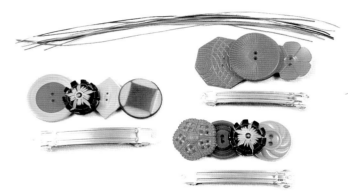

Selecting materials.

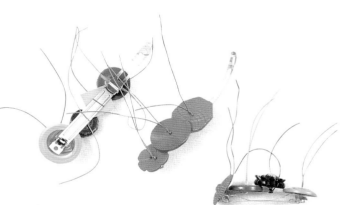

Tying buttons on a clip with colored phone wire.

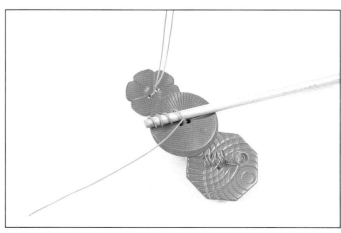

Coiling the phone wire.

Using hot glue to keep buttons in place.

Elastic Button Bracelet

STEP ONE Lay out buttons in the order you want them around your wrist. Consider varying colors and textures.

STEP TWO Starting from the back of the first button, thread the elastic through two holes in each button.

STEP THREE Adjust the buttons so they overlap and make sure the elastic is taut but not stretched out.

STEP FOUR Tie the ends of the elastic into a knot. Drop a dot of cyanoacrylate glue on the knot and let it dry.

STEP FIVE Clip the ends of the elastic fairly close to the knot.

MATERIALS

Eight to nine ⁷⁄₈″ to 1¹⁄₈″ two- or four-hole buttons (shank buttons do not work well for this project)

9″ piece of thin black elastic cord

Cyanoacrylate glue

TOOLS

Scissors

▶ *Elastic Button Bracelets using interestingly shaped and textured buttons.*

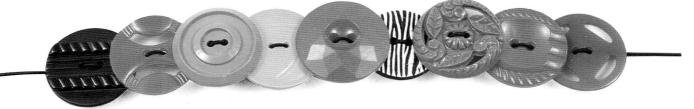

Stringing elastic cord through the buttons.

Tying the knot.

Electrically Connected Earrings

STEP ONE Wrap purple wire around the rubber gaskets, as shown. Trim the end of the wire.

STEP TWO Put a piece of green wire through one of the blue beads and twist as shown.

STEP THREE Drill a hole in the top of the wire connector.

STEP FOUR Take the green wire up though the center of the wire connector and through the hole.

STEP FIVE Place the wrapped gasket over the top of the wire connector.

STEP SIX Put a green bead on the wire.

STEP SEVEN Loop the green wire twice around the round-nose pliers, ⅛″ above the top of the wire connector. Then bring the wire down and wrap the wire around the back, toward the top of the wire connector.

STEP EIGHT Cut the end of the wire and attach the ear wire through the double loop.

MATERIALS

2	¾″-long orange electrical wire connectors
2	1″ rubber gaskets
2	8mm round green beads
2	10mm round blue beads
2	18″-long pieces of purple phone wire
2	12″-long pieces of green phone wire
2	ear wires

TOOLS

Round-nose pliers
Needle-nose pliers
Wire cutters
Drill or Dremel

Steps for assembling Electrically Connected Earrings.

Electrically Connected Earrings made of wire connectors, rubber gaskets, beads, colored phone wire and base metal findings.

Resistor Earrings

Adding beads to the resistor wires.

STEP ONE Put beads on the wires of the resistors.

STEP TWO Bend the wire over at the end of the last bead. Trim if necessary and form an eye loop.

STEP THREE Put a jump ring through the eye loops and close it.

STEP FOUR Attach the ear wire to the jump ring.

ANOTHER OPTION

STEP ONE Attach one beaded resistor wire to the ear wire. Fold the other beaded resistor wire over the front of the resistor at an angle.

STEP TWO Form an eye loop at the end of the folded wire.

STEP THREE Put a few beads on a head pin and attach it to the free loop. (Notice the red earring.)

MATERIALS
2 interesting resistors with two wires on the same side
A variety of beads
Ear wires
Jump ring

TOOLS
Round-nose pliers
Needle-nose pliers
Wire cutters

▶ *Two different Resistor Earrings made of electronic resistors and beads with base metal findings.*

Hardware Charm Necklace

STEP ONE Add small resistors to the 2″ circuit board by putting the ends in existing holes or drilled holes, or wrapping them in among the pins. Put a jump ring in the corner.

STEP TWO Loop the spring so the ends meet, and connect them with a wire or resistor.

STEP THREE Make eye loops in the ends of the wires of the resistors.

STEP FOUR Lay out pieces in an interesting order. Start with the center piece and work your way out. Match the left side to the right side for visual balance.

STEP FIVE With a jump ring, attach the center piece to the ball chain between the balls. Then attach all other pieces, making sure they are evenly spaced.

STEP SIX Attach the ball chain ends to each end of the chain.

STEP SEVEN Attach a split ring to the clasp and attach it to one end of the chain.

MATERIALS

2   2″-long springs
1   2″-square circuit board part
Plastic doodads
A variety of different resistors—at least 2 of each
24″ ball chain
2   ball chain ends with loops
A few jump rings
1   spring ring
1   claw clasp

TOOLS

Needle-nose pliers
Round-nose pliers
Wire cutters

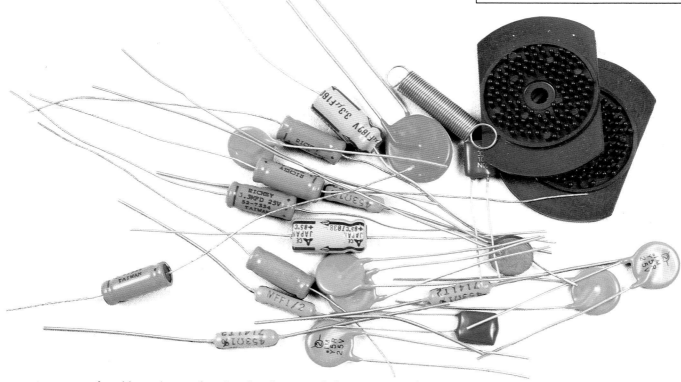

A variety of necklace charms found in hardware and electronics supply stores.

*Hardware Charm Necklace using a
variety of electronic parts, ball chain
and base metal findings.*

Fancy Resistor & Bead Necklace

STEP ONE Cut one wire off of each resistor.

STEP TWO File the cut ends so they are no longer sharp.

STEP THREE Cut the remaining wire on the $^9/_{16}$″ resistors to 1$^1/_4$″ long.

STEP FOUR Cut the remaining wire on the $^1/_4$″ resistors to varying lengths from $^7/_8$″ to 1$^1/_4$″.

STEP FIVE Make eye loops on all resistors to prepare for stringing.

STEP SIX Set aside fourteen small, prepared resistors for the earrings. Try to select pairs by color and length.

STEP SEVEN Lay out fourteen small, prepared resistors between single large resistors.

STEP EIGHT String the resistors onto leather cord first, then string the glass beads going up either side.

STEP NINE On one end of the cord, attach a split ring. On the other end, attach the clasp. (See the wire wrapping technique on page 13.)

Preparing the resistors for stringing.

STEP TEN Start making the earrings by putting seven prepared resistors on a jump ring for each one.

STEP ELEVEN On each eye pin put one blue bead and one gold bead. Make an eye loop.

STEP TWELVE To one end of the eye loop attach the jump ring with the resistors, and on the other end attach the ear wire.

MATERIALS	
8	$^9/_{16}$″-long resistors with wire coming out of both ends
140	$^1/_4$″-long resistors in a variety of colors
26	6mm round gold iridescent round beads
16	10mm round blue beads
12	10mm round purple beads
	24″-long thin leather cord
	6″ to 8″ of 24-gauge sterling wire
1	7mm split ring
	Clasp
2	eye pins
2	jump rings
2	ear wires

TOOLS

Needle-nose pliers
Round-nose pliers
Wire cutters
Metal file

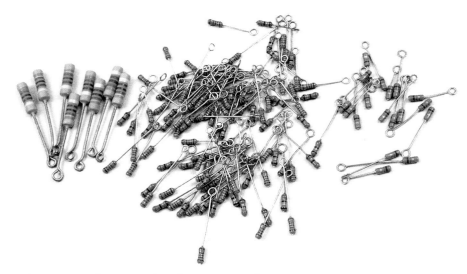

Resistors with various-length wires—ready to go.

Resistor & Bead Necklace using electronic resistors, beads, tiger tail and base metal findings.

Cable Tie Earrings & Pin

STEP ONE Interlock the cable ties. Put a red into a blue, into a yellow, into a green, into the red to form a square. (See first photo.) Do all three sets and put one aside.

STEP TWO Take two interlocked pieces and, using the wire cutters, trim the red, blue and green pieces to 1½″ long. Trim the yellow to 1¼″. Save the scraps.

STEP THREE Drill holes in the end of each piece.

STEP FOUR Bend the blue and green pieces down away from the red piece a half-inch from the end.

STEP FIVE With the scraps, cut two each of the green, blue and yellow to 2¼″ long. Drill holes in each end.

STEP SIX Hook the 7mm jump rings through each end of the 2¼″ pieces, forming a loop. (See second photo.)

STEP SEVEN Attach the green loop to the blue end, the red loop to the yellow end and the blue loop to the green end.

STEP EIGHT Place the 7mm jump ring through the red end at the top and attach the ear wire.

STEP NINE For the pin, take the third interlocked section and trim the red to 4⅜″, the blue to 3⅛″, the yellow to 2½″ and the green to 3¼″.

STEP TEN Drill the ends of each piece and loop onto the 10mm jump ring as shown. (See third photo.)

MATERIALS

3 each—red, blue, yellow, and green self-locking cable ties
8 7mm jump rings
1 10mm jump ring
2 ear wires
12″ red phone wire
1 1″ pin back

TOOLS

Drill or Dremel
Needle-nose pliers
Wire cutters

STEP ELEVEN Wrap the pin back halfway with the phone wire, then loop down and tie in the jump ring. Bring the wire back up and finish wrapping.

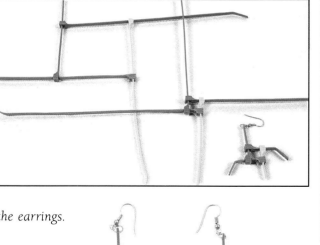

Photo 1.
Interlocking colors for the earrings and pin.

Photo 2.
Steps to constructing the earrings.

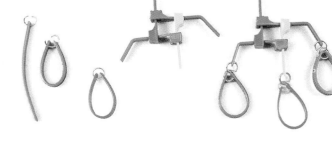

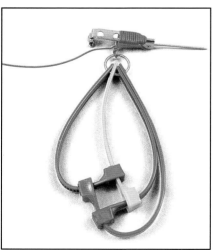

Photo 3.
Constructing the pin.

Cable Tie Earrings & Pin made of brightly colored self-locking cable ties and base metal findings.

Fabric Covered Gasket Pin & Earrings

TO MAKE THE EARRINGS:

STEP ONE Drill a hole in each 1″ gasket halfway from the edge to the center hole.

STEP TWO Put a 6mm round bead on the head pin and put it through the drilled hole in the gasket. Fold the pin up against the gasket.

STEP THREE Add an 8mm rondelle, a cylinder bead and a 6mm round bead on the head pin, so they all rest on top of the gasket.

STEP FOUR Finish off the head pin and attach it to the ear wires.

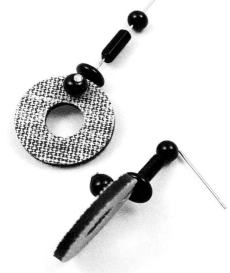

Putting the earrings together with a head pin and beads.

MATERIALS

2	1″ fabric-covered rubber gaskets
2	1⅜″ fabric-covered rubber gaskets
2	ear wires
5	head pins
5	6mm round black beads
2	6mm black rondelles (a flattened, "disk-shaped" round bead)
3	8mm black rondelles
4	10mm black cylinder beads
1	8mm round black bead
1	triangular black bead
1	1″ pin back
Cyanoacrylate glue	

TOOLS

Needle-nose pliers
Round-nose pliers
Drill or Dremel

The back of the pin, showing how to finish off the head pin and where to place the pin back.

TO MAKE THE PIN:

STEP ONE Glue the two 1⅜″ gaskets together so that the outer edge of the top one touches the edge of the inner hole of the bottom one.

STEP TWO Drill two holes on the right-hand side of these two gaskets, ½″ apart and ⅛″ from the outer edge.

STEP THREE For the lower left hole put an 8mm bead and a cylinder bead on a head pin. Bend the pin 90°. Put a 6mm rondelle on the head pin and put it through the hole. On the back of the pin, create an eye loop and then press it flat against the gasket.

STEP FOUR Glue on the pin back with cyanoacrylate glue. (See the photo at left, bottom, for the location.)

STEP FIVE From the back of the gasket, put a head pin through the upper right hole. Add a 6mm rondelle and bend the pin 90°. Add a cylinder bead and an 8mm rondelle, then make an eye loop.

STEP SIX On another head pin, put a 6mm round bead and the triangular bead. Make an eye loop and attach it to the other eye loop.

▶ *Fabric Covered Gasket Pin & Earrings with glass beads and base metal findings.*

Brass Gasket Earrings

STEP ONE With the fine-point marker, mark the bottom edge of the gasket at five spots, ¹⁄₁₆″ from the edge and ½″ apart. Then mark two spots on the top edge of the gasket, opposite the middle mark you made on the bottom, ¹⁄₁₆″ from the outer edge and ¹⁄₁₆″ from the center.

STEP TWO Use the nail set to start the holes, then drill.

STEP THREE File off the burrs around the holes.

STEP FOUR Stack beads on the head pins in the order shown below and make an eye loop.

STEP FIVE Attach each head pin with beads to the holes in the bottom of the gasket using the jump rings.

STEP SIX Add a large, special bead to a head pin with a cobalt blue rondelle at either end. Form an eye loop, attach it to a jump ring and put it through the center hole, so it hangs into the negative space of the gasket.

STEP SEVEN Add an ear wire to the top of the gasket using a jump ring.

MATERIALS

2	1¾″ brass gaskets
14	7mm brass jump rings
12	brass head pins
2	brass ear wires
10	light blue rondelles
4	6mm cobalt blue rondelles
2	8mm cobalt blue rondelles
2	15mm × 10mm special cobalt blue bead

TOOLS

Drill/Dremel
Fine-tooth file or emery paper
Needle-nose pliers
Round-nose pliers
Nail set
Fine-point marker

Parts and holes ready for the earrings.

▶ *Brass Gasket Earrings embellished with glass beads.*

Folded Window Screen Earrings & Pin

TO MAKE THE EARRINGS:

STEP ONE Cut four pieces of screen approximately 1¼" square.

STEP TWO Line up two pieces on top of each other. Stitch the bottoms together with yellow embroidery floss. Leave excess thread beyond the edges of the screen.

STEP THREE Stitch the left side with green and the right side with blue.

STEP FOUR Open the screen packet, and fold it so that the blue and the green thread line up and stitch the edge closed with the red thread.

STEP FIVE Trim all thread to approximately ½" long.

STEP SIX Attach an ear wire with a jump ring in the center of the yellow edge.

TO MAKE THE PIN:

STEP SEVEN Cut out two pieces of screen approximately 1¾" square.

STEP EIGHT Repeat Steps Two through Five of the earring procedure.

STEP NINE Press the screen flat and lay the button on one side and put the pin back on the other. Stitch the button to the pin back through the screen.

MATERIALS

Scraps of black vinyl window screen
Embroidery floss in yellow, red, green and blue
1 special glass button
2 7mm jump rings
2 ear wires
1 3/4" pin back
Button thread

TOOLS

Scissors
Embroidery needle (or any large-hole sewing needle)
Needle-nose pliers

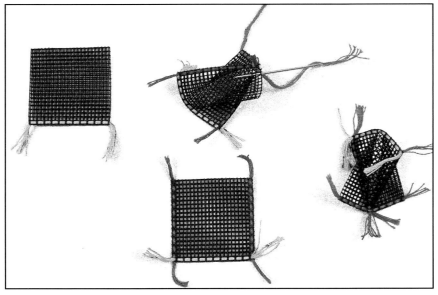

Sewing the screen together with embroidery floss.

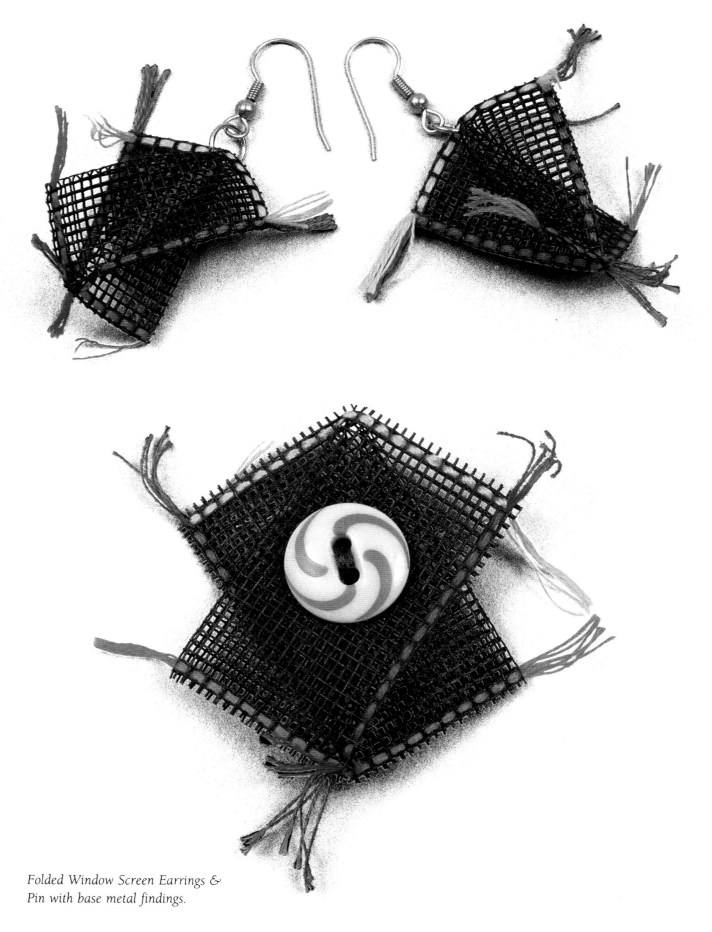

Folded Window Screen Earrings &
Pin with base metal findings.

Faucet Strainer Earrings & Necklace

TO MAKE THE EARRINGS:

STEP ONE With the straight pin, make a hole in the centers of the strainers large enough to get the head pin through.

STEP TWO Place beads and a strainer on the head pins in the order shown below.

Layout of earring components.

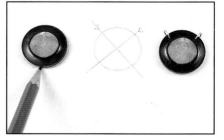

How to determine where to drill holes in the strainers for the necklace.

Step Five layout of beads on eye pins for the necklace.

STEP THREE Make an eye loop on the end of each head pin and attach them to the ear wires.

TO MAKE THE NECKLACE:

STEP ONE Trace a faucet strainer on paper and divide the circle in half and then in quarters as shown. Draw lines across the rim of each strainer where the arrows indicate.

STEP TWO Drill holes in the center of the rims on the lines you have drawn on the strainers.

STEP THREE In the strainer that will be in the center of the necklace, and which will have another strainer hanging from it, drill four holes.

STEP FOUR Place jump rings in the holes of the strainers.

STEP FIVE String beads on eye pins as shown (see photo, bottom left).

STEP SIX Make an eye loop on the end of the eye pins, making sure each one lines up horizontally with the other end of the eye pin.

STEP SEVEN Attach beaded eye pins to the strainers in the order shown on the finished piece.

STEP EIGHT Attach a split ring on each end and attach the clasp to the right side split ring.

MATERIALS

For the Necklace

12	faucet strainers
6	8mm round red beads
4	8mm round black beads
8	8mm red rondelles
16	8mm black rondelles
10	red cylinder beads
6	black cylinder beads
14	eye pins
26	7mm jump rings
2	6mm split rings
1	spring ring or lobster claw clasp

For the Earrings

2	faucet strainers
4	8mm red round beads
2	8mm black round beads
2	10mm black rondelles
2	red cylinder beads
2	black cylinder beads
2	head pins
2	ear wires

TOOLS

Paper
Pencil
Needle- or chain-nose pliers
Round-nose pliers
Drill or Dremel with 1/32" drill bit
Straight pin

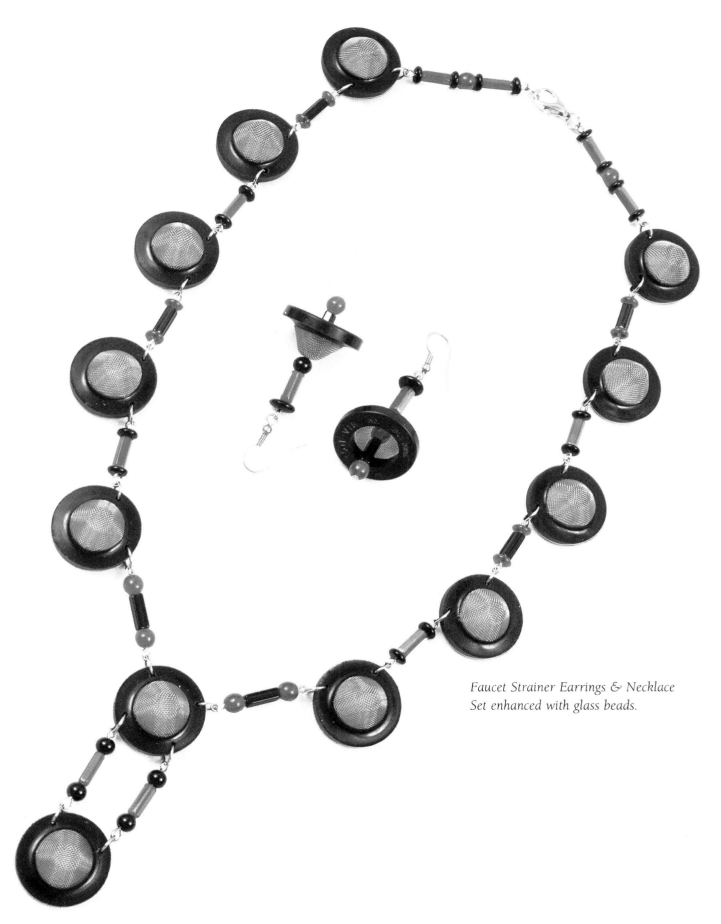

Faucet Strainer Earrings & Necklace Set enhanced with glass beads.

Anodized Aluminum Pin & Earrings

TO MAKE THE PIN:

STEP ONE Cut the red sheet so it is 1⅛″ high on one end and leave the other end at 1¼″.

STEP TWO Gently roll up the narrow end of the purple triangle using the round-nosed pliers covered with masking tape. Make sure the purple triangle will fit on the red trapezoid.

STEP THREE Glue the purple triangle onto the red trapezoid with cyanoacrylate glue. Use very little glue.

STEP FOUR Drill holes in the two corners of the triangle through both layers of aluminum.

STEP FIVE Put a 10mm cobalt rondelle on a head pin and put the rondelle through the bottom hole of the pin from the front. Bend down the back of the pin and add a yellow rondelle, a round green bead and an orange rondelle. Make an eye loop so that the beads hang down just below the edge of the red aluminum.

STEP SIX On another head pin put

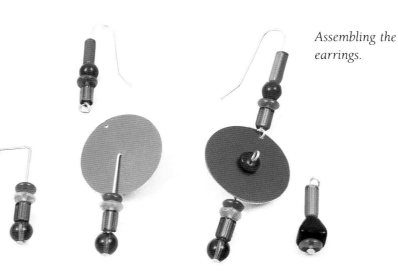

Assembling the earrings.

a turquoise rondelle and a triangle bead and attach this to the eye loop formed in Step Five.

STEP SEVEN Put a 4mm turquoise bead on a head pin and put it through the other hole from the front side. Add a cobalt rondelle and bend the head pin down. Add an 8mm round purple bead. Hang this below the pin and make an eye loop.

STEP EIGHT On another head pin put a round turquoise bead and a red rondelle and attach it to the eye loop formed in Step Seven.

STEP NINE Glue the pin back on with cyanoacrylate glue.

TO MAKE THE EARRINGS:

STEP ONE Drill one hole in the center of each disk and another hole ¹⁄₁₆″ in from the edge.

STEP TWO On two head pins, stack a round purple bead, a 6mm green cylinder bead, a yellow

rondelle and a red rondelle. Bend the head pin ½″ above the top of the red bead and put the end of the head pin through the center hole of the disk. Add a cobalt rondelle and then form an eye loop.

STEP THREE On two head pins stack a turquoise rondelle, a black triangle bead and a gold cylinder bead. Form an eye loop and attach it to the eye loop formed in Step Two.

STEP FOUR On the long ear wires, add a red cylinder bead, a round cobalt bead, a red rondelle and a green cylinder bead. Form an eye loop and attach it to the top hole in the disk.

Note: *Anodized aluminum scratches easily, so keep the protective plastic coating on until you are ready to attach the beads. Gently file off any burrs that develop during the sawing.*

A view of the back of the pin.

MATERIALS

For the Earrings

2	1″ red anodized aluminum disks
2	long sterling French ear wires
2	sterling head pins
2	black triangle beads
2	6mm orange rondelles
2	6mm red rondelles
2	6mm yellow rondelles
2	6mm turquoise rondelles
2	6mm cobalt rondelles
2	10mm red cylinder beads
2	10mm golden cylinder beads
4	6mm cylinder beads
2	6mm round cobalt beads
2	6mm round purple beads

For the Pin

1	2″ × 1¼″ piece of red anodized aluminum sheet
1	triangular piece of purple anodized aluminum sheet approximately 2¼″ long
3	sterling head pins
1	base pin back
1	10mm cobalt rondelle
1	6mm cobalt rondelle
1	6mm yellow rondelle
1	6mm orange rondelle
1	6mm red rondelle
1	6mm turquoise rondelle
1	8mm round purple bead
1	6mm round green bead
2	4mm round cobalt beads
1	black triangular bead

Masking tape
Cyanoacrylate glue

TOOLS

Jeweler's saw
Needle-nose pliers
Round-nose pliers
File
Drill or Dremel

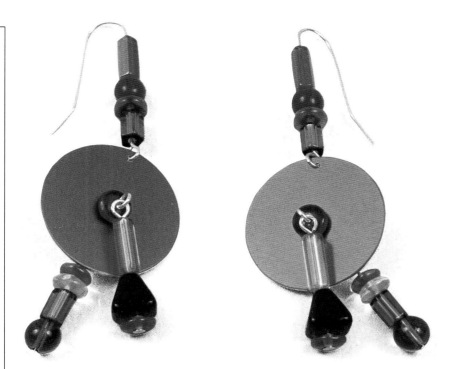

Anodized Aluminum Pin & Earrings incorporating glass beads and sterling findings.

Gallery of Found Objects & Hardware Jewelry

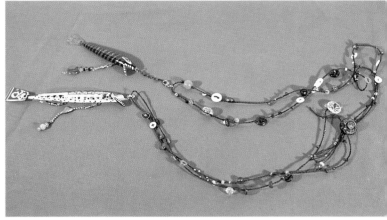

Cam Harper, Chicago, IL
Cosmic Cartographer
Fishing lure, paint, paper, charms, waxed linen, found objects, vintage buttons, beads
©1994

Sheila Dehner, New York, NY
Button Necklace #7
1950s plastic, brass, bakelite
19"
©1992

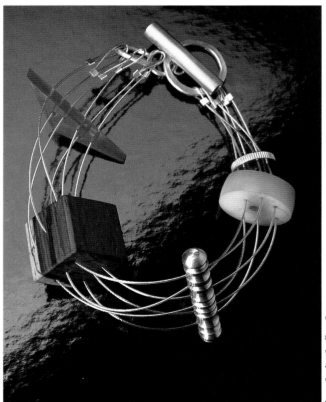

Ann Jenkins & Bill Keith, Bar Harbor, ME
Bracelet
Nylon-coated steel cable, plexiglass, wood, aluminum, copal amber, brass
2" × 7½" × ¾"
©1993

Photo Credit: Geoffrey Carr

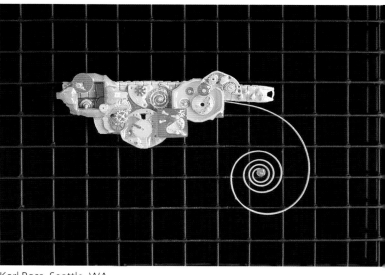

Karl Ross, Seattle, WA
Timely Revivals
Watch parts
5"
©1988

Miriam Salzer, San Francisco, CA
Tone/Volume Bolos
Mixed media
18½" × 1" × ¾"
©1991

Patricia Meyerowitz, Easton, PA
Pendant and chain
Brass
2¾" × 3"
Mid-1970s

Chapter Three

PAPER, FIBER AND WOOD

Paper is a versatile material—it can be folded, crinkled, glued and painted. The paper used in these projects ranges from scraps of gift wrap to handmade paper. It is pretty easy to find interesting papers in your local art supply stores. Also check craft shows and local galleries to see if there are paper makers in your area. If so, they usually sell paper by the sheet.

The fiber in these projects ranges from Poly-fil to wonderfully patterned fabric. You will probably be able to find scraps of fabric in your own home, your parent's home or a friend's home. We all know someone who has a stash of fabric scraps whether they make clothes, quilts or fiber art.

Wood is a bit more durable than paper or fiber and usually requires some painting, dyeing, staining or sealing. The basswood used in these projects is fairly lightweight and easily cut with a jeweler's saw. Once you have mastered the complex cutting of the hands in the project on pages 68-69, you'll be ready to cut any shape.

Collage Paper Pins

The steps for gluing paper onto the foam core.

STEP ONE Cut a 2″ square of foam core with the knife.

STEP TWO Cut the paper 3½″ square and trim as shown above.

STEP THREE Place the foam core over the paper and adjust it to fit exactly the way you want it. Fold the paper around the foam core, making strong creases. Remove the foam core.

STEP FOUR Put glue on one side of the foam core, then place the foam core in the center of the back side of the creased paper and press down carefully.

STEP FIVE Put glue on the edges and part of the back of the foam core and fold the paper over and rub down.

STEP SIX Cut a 1⅞″-square piece of paper for the back. Glue it onto the back of the foam core.

STEP SEVEN Collage any other pieces of paper on the front of the pin at this time.

STEP EIGHT Attach the pin back with hot glue.

Note: *If you wish to make these pieces more durable, you can use an acrylic sealer. If you use a sealer, you will be able to make collage paper earrings. However, you will lose some of the texture and the soft look of the paper.*

MATERIALS

Foam core
Interesting papers
White glue
1   ½″ pin back
Hot glue

TOOLS

Scissors
Utility knife
Glue gun
Ruler

OPTIONAL

Acrylic sealer

▶ *Collage Paper Pins using handmade paper, straight magazine photos and collaged magazine images.*

Folded Gift Paper Pin & Earrings

TO MAKE THE EARRINGS:

STEP ONE Cut three pieces of gift wrap to 2½″ × 4⅞″.

STEP TWO Cut a piece of mat board to 2½″ × 1¼″.

STEP THREE Carefully fanfold two of the pieces of paper.

STEP FOUR Cut one piece of the paper in half so it is 1¼″ × 4⅞″.

STEP FIVE With one of the half-pieces, start gluing the fan sections together by only gluing the back side of the paper to itself. (See the photo above, right.) It works well to start from the center and work toward the ends. Stop just before you glue the ends together.

STEP SIX Put two rondelles on a head pin and bend the pin at 1¼″ plus the thickness of the two beads. Form an eye loop.

STEP SEVEN Set the head pin in the center of the glued fan. Put one rondelle on top of the fan and one on the bottom and glue the paper ends together. Attach this to the ear wire.

STEP EIGHT Repeat Steps Five through Seven for the other earring.

Forming the fan for the earrings.

TO MAKE THE PIN:

STEP ONE Take the last fanfolded piece of paper and glue one end to one edge of the mat board and the other end to the other edge of the mat board.

STEP TWO Roll the third piece of paper into a ⅝″-diameter cylinder and glue it.

STEP THREE Put a thin line of glue the long way down the cylinder and set it on the mat board under the fan-folded piece. Let dry.

STEP FOUR Hot-glue the pin back to the top narrow edge of the back.

MATERIALS
Interesting gift wrap
Black mat board
White glue
Hot glue
2   head pins
2   ear wires
4   6mm rondelles
1   1″ pin back
TOOLS
Mat knife
Ruler
Round-nose pliers
Needle-nose pliers
Glue gun

Forming the fan for the pin.

▶ *Folded Gift Paper Pin & Earrings.*

Sponge-Painted Paper Hearts

STEP ONE Sponge-paint one side of the paper. Do all of the colors—one at a time—except for the white. Let the paint dry between layers.

STEP TWO Sponge-paint the back of the paper. Let it dry.

STEP THREE Tear the masking tape so it has ragged edges, and lightly lay it down in stripes on the paper at a diagonal approximately ½″ apart.

STEP FOUR Sponge-paint with white on top of the untaped areas. Lay the paint on fairly heavily. Pull off the tape carefully and let the paint dry. Do not leave the tape on or it will not be removeable unless you tear the paper.

STEP FIVE Repeat Steps Three and Four on the other side of the paper.

STEP SIX With scrap paper, make a heart pattern for the earrings and one larger and one smaller for the pin.

STEP SEVEN Trace one small, one large and three medium hearts on the painted paper. Cut them out.

STEP EIGHT With a black marker, outline all the hearts, front and back.

STEP NINE With a needle, punch a hole in two of the medium hearts, then add a jump ring and ear wire.

STEP TEN Lay out the remaining hearts in an interesting arrangement and glue or sew them together.

STEP ELEVEN With a needle, punch a hole in the largest heart and attach the safety pin with a jump ring.

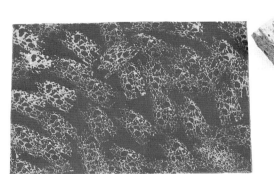

The first layer of sponge painting.

MATERIALS

Sheet of black cover stock (heavy paper)
Masking tape
4 to 5 different colors of acrylic paint plus white
Scrap paper
Permanent black marker
2   gold-colored ear wires
2   gold-colored safety pins
Button thread
4   7mm gold-colored jump rings
White glue

TOOLS

Scissors
Sponge for painting
Sewing needle

Masking the paper for the final layer of paint.

▶ *Sponge-Painted Paper Hearts with gold-colored findings.*

Layered Tissue Paper Earrings & Pin

STEP ONE Cut one piece of foam core 3″ × 1¼″, and two pieces 1¼″ × 1¼″.

STEP TWO Tear the colored tissue in strips long enough to wrap to the back of the piece, and lay them out so they will overlap on the foam core.

STEP THREE Put Mod Podge on top of one piece of foam core and lay down tissue on top of it. Smooth with a brush covered with Mod Podge. (Tissue color will run, so brush each color individually and rinse the brush between colors.)

STEP FOUR Glue tissue around the sides to the back. Set this aside to dry.

STEP FIVE Repeat Steps Two through Four for the other pieces.

STEP SIX Cut two pieces of white tissue 2″ × 2″ and one piece 4″ × 2¼″.

STEP SEVEN Glue down white tissue on each piece and wrap it around to the back. Fold the corners like you would when wrapping a gift.

STEP EIGHT Cut two pieces of the darkest colors a little less than

Laying out and gluing torn tissue on foam core.

1¼″ × 1¼″ and glue these on the backs of the earring pieces.

STEP NINE Cut one piece of the darkest color a little less than 4″ × 2¼″ and glue this on the back of the pin piece.

STEP TEN Tear narrow strips of tissue to correspond to the colors on the first layer. Make these long enough so they will touch in the back, especially on the earring shapes.

STEP ELEVEN Glue strips on top of the matching color of the first layer. Do the front sides first and let these dry, then glue them to the back.

STEP TWELVE Completely seal the pieces with Mod Podge.

STEP THIRTEEN Hot-glue the pin back on the large piece.

STEP FOURTEEN For the earrings, use the pin to poke a hole through the thickness of the foam core from corner to corner so the earrings hang facing out at a diagonal.

STEP FIFTEEN Insert the head pin, bend it carefully, create an eye loop and attach it to the ear wire.

The second layer using white tissue and the third layer of repeated color.

MATERIALS
6 or 7 colors of tissue paper plus white
Foam core
1½″ pin back
2 head pins
2 ear wires
Matte-finish Mod Podge or other acrylic glue/sealer
Hot glue

TOOLS
Mat knife
Paint brush
Scissors
Glue gun
2″-long T-pin or needle
Bowl of water to rinse brush
Needle-nose pliers
Round-nose pliers

▶ *Layered Tissue Paper Earrings & Pin on foam core using acrylic sealer with base metal findings.*

Fabric Collage Pins

STEP ONE Cut foam core to the desired size.

STEP TWO Cut a piece of fabric large enough to cover the front of the foam core and wrap to the back of the foam core.

STEP THREE Glue fabric to the foam core with the white glue using the same technique as for the Collage Paper Pins on page 46.

STEP FOUR Cut a piece of the same fabric slightly smaller than the base and glue it to the back.

STEP FIVE Cut two to three pieces of the other fabrics so they fit on the base.

STEP SIX Fringe the fabric by removing some of the end threads from all four sides.

STEP SEVEN Put a drop of Fray Check on each corner to prevent extra threads from coming loose.

STEP EIGHT Glue the fringed pieces on the base in an interesting layout. Just put glue in the center of the piece and let the fringe remain loose.

Note: *Because we have not sealed the fabric, this technique does not work well for earrings.*

MATERIALS
3 different loosely woven fabrics
Foam core
White glue
Fray Check
Hot glue
Pin back

TOOLS
Scissors
Glue gun

Fabric in various stages of preparation.

Fabric Collage Pins utilizing some scraps from the closet.

Rolled Ribbon Earrings & Pin

Wrapping ribbons on a dowel rod for earrings, and forming the pin on a flat surface while they are wet.

MATERIALS

Colorful fabric ribbon ⅞" to 1" wide
Stiffy fabric stiffener
2   7mm jump rings
2   ear wires
1   1" pin back

TOOLS

Paint brush
⅜" dowel rod covered with plastic
    wrap
Plastic wrap
Scissors
T-pin

TO MAKE THE EARRINGS:

STEP ONE   Cut a 6" length of ribbon, then cut it in half lengthwise.

STEP TWO   Either dip or paint one of the 6" pieces of ribbon with Stiffy (follow the directions on the bottle) until the fabric is saturated. Remove the excess stiffener.

STEP THREE   Spiral wrap the ribbon around the plastic-wrapped dowel rod. Set this aside to dry. Try not to let it touch anything as it is drying. Repeat with the second 6" length.

STEP FOUR   Pierce a hole in one end of each of the 6" spirals. Add a jump ring and ear wire.

TO MAKE THE PIN:

STEP ONE   Cut a 4¼" length of ribbon. Dip or paint with Stiffy. Twist the ribbon and lay it on a flat piece of plastic wrap as shown. Let this dry.

STEP TWO   Hot-glue the pin back onto the ribbon twist.

▶ *Rolled Ribbon Earrings & Pin using Stiffy fabric stiffener.*

Embellished Pillow Pins

STEP ONE Cut two fabric squares measuring 2½". Cut these as square to the grain as possible.

STEP TWO Fringe the ends of the squares approximately ⅜" to ½" in from the edges. This will give you a fairly accurate square.

STEP THREE Lay the two pieces back to back. Stitch around three sides as close to the edge of the fringe as possible. Leave 2" of thread at both ends of the stitching.

STEP FOUR Thread the bead needle and tie a knot at the end of the thread. Put the needle inside the pillow and push it out through the front. Pull the thread taut and leave it for the moment.

STEP FIVE Stuff the pillow with Poly-fil.

STEP SIX Stitch the pillow closed. Again, leave 2" of thread at both ends of the stitching.

STEP SEVEN Tie the corner threads into knots. Individually thread each onto a needle, sew it back into the pillow and out the other side, and clip. This hides all of

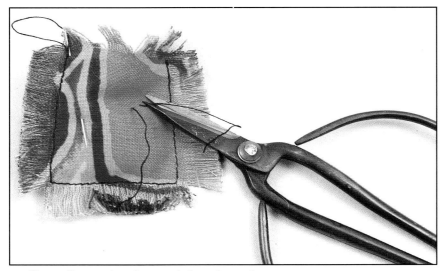

Stuffing pillow and tucking end threads inside.

the extra threads.

STEP EIGHT Sew beads on the front of the pillow using the nylon thread you attached. Pick up a bead and stitch it to the pillow and come out in a different place. Continue until you have ran-domly covered the pillow with approximately 30 beads.

STEP NINE As you sew on the last bead, push the needle through to the back of the pillow and sew on the pin back.

STEP TEN Trim fringe if necessary.

MATERIALS

Interesting scraps of patterned fabric
Multicolored small beads—
 approximately 30 per pin
Pin back
Poly-fil
Nylon beading thread

TOOLS

Sewing machine or needle and
 thread
Scissors
Bead needle

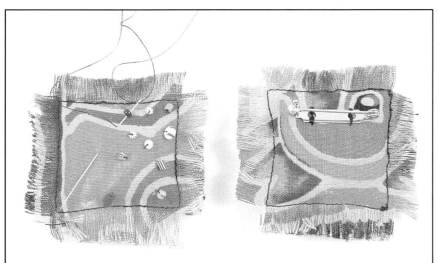

Sewing beads on, and the pin back sewn on.

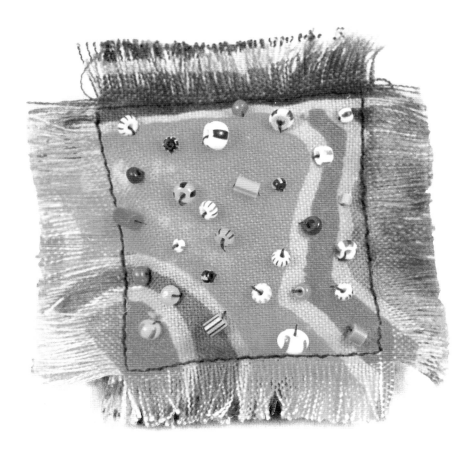

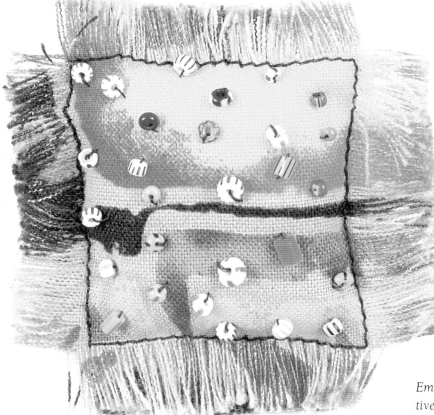

Embellished Pillow Pins using decorative beads.

Poly-fil Bead Necklace & Earrings

TO MAKE THE NECKLACE:

STEP ONE Lay two sheets of vinyl together and cut out 7 odd shapes, approximately 2″ in size.

STEP TWO Stitch three-fourths of the way around each double piece shape. Make the shape no bigger than 1½″ in any direction. Leave long threads at the beginning and end of the stitching. After this step is done, do Steps Three through Five on one shape at a time.

STEP THREE Stuff the shape approximately half full with Poly-fil. Put in a few pinches of the seed beads. Fill up the rest of the shape with Poly-fil. Tuck it in really well.

STEP FOUR Stitch the shape closed. Again, leave the threads long at both ends of the stitching. Tie the threads in each corner to each other to keep the stitching from unraveling.

STEP FIVE Trim the vinyl to within ⅛″ of the stitching.

STEP SIX Lay the cord out and place the shapes in an interesting order. Leaving about ½″ between shapes, tie them onto the cord. Put a drop of Fray Check on each knot.

STEP SEVEN Trim the cord to a length you find comfortable. Put a crimp on each end of the cord (see technique on page 12). Add a jump ring to both ends and the clasp onto one end.

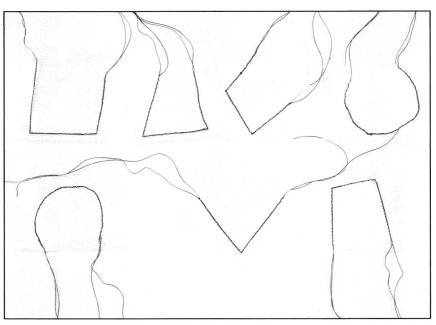

Shapes for the necklace sewn three-quarters of the way around and ready for stuffing.

TO MAKE THE EARRINGS:

STEP ONE Cut from the doubled vinyl two shapes that match (this will give you four matching shapes). Complete Steps Two through Five of the necklace procedure.

STEP TWO On the inside of the stitching, pierce a hole in one corner of each piece with the T-pin. Insert a jump ring and attach the ear wire.

Stuffed shapes ready to tie onto the cord.

MATERIALS
Clear vinyl sheet (approximately 2′ square)
Poly-fil
Black glass seed beads (tiny beads usually used for bead embroidery)
24″ thin leather cord
4   7mm jump rings
2   ear wires
1   clasp
2   crimps
Fray Check
Cyanoacrylate glue
TOOLS
Sewing machine
T-pin

▶ *Poly-fil Bead Necklace & Earrings, using the threads as an added element.*

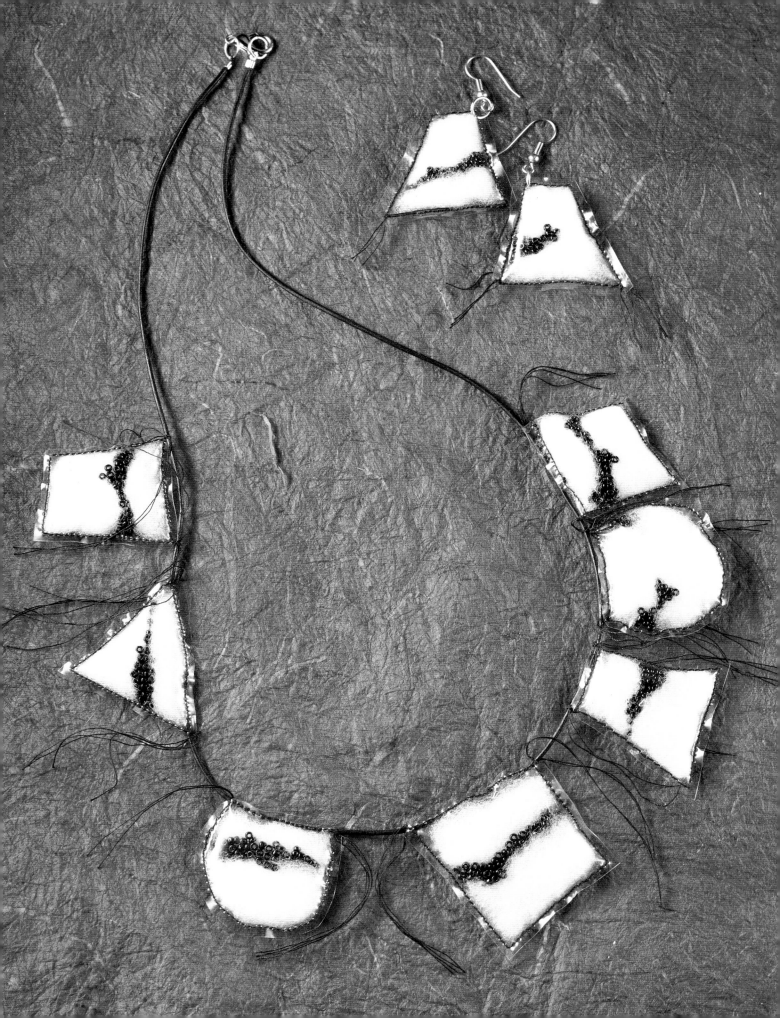

Woodsie Earrings & Pin

MATERIALS

Woodsie brand shapes
2 ear wires
2 7mm jump rings
1 1″ pin back
4 colors of acrylic paint
White glue
Hot glue

TOOLS

Paint brush
Drill or Dremel
Glue gun

STEP ONE Choose five ovals or circles that are the same size—approximately 1½″ in the longest direction. Choose three smaller pieces the same shape.

STEP TWO Paint the front sides of the large shapes one color. Let them dry and then paint the backs the same color.

STEP THREE Paint the three small shapes the same color—one side only.

STEP FOUR Paint the last two large shapes two different colors—both sides.

STEP FIVE For each earring, use white glue to secure one small shape on the corner or on the edge of a larger shape.

STEP SIX Choose the top of each shape and drill a hole. Add a jump ring and ear wire.

STEP SEVEN For the pin, glue the remaining large pieces in a fanned out pattern.

STEP EIGHT Glue the last small shape on the top piece close to the edge. (See below.)

STEP NINE Hot-glue the pin back in place.

Selecting Woodsie shapes to use.

Woodsie Earrings & Pin painted with acrylic paint.

Constructed Wood Pin

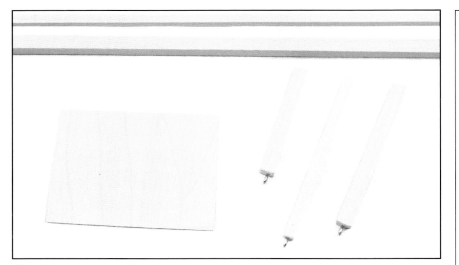

Wood shapes cut and ready to paint.

MATERIALS

⅛"-thick basswood sheet (found at
    hardware or craft stores)
³⁄₁₆"-square basswood rod
⅛"-square basswood rod
3   ⅛" screw eyes
3   head pins
2   8mm round beads
1   8mm rondelle
2   6mm round beads
3   6mm rondelles
4 colors of acrylic paint
1   1½" pin back
White glue
Hot glue

TOOLS

Jeweler's saw
Drill or Dremel
Sandpaper
Paint brush
Glue gun
Round-nose pliers
Needle-nose pliers

STEP ONE   Cut a 2" × 1½" rectangle out of the basswood sheet; sand the edges.

STEP TWO   Cut two pieces of ³⁄₁₆" rod, one 2" long and one 1½" long. Sand the edges.

STEP THREE   Cut one piece of ⅛" rod 2¼" long. Sand the edges.

STEP FOUR   Drill a hole in the bottom end of each cut rod.

STEP FIVE   Put a dab of white glue on the end of each screw eye and insert them in each of the drilled holes.

STEP SIX   Paint each piece of wood (rods and flat piece) a different color and let them dry. Apply a second coat if necessary.

STEP SEVEN   Glue rods onto the flat piece with screw eyes all facing down. Vary the heights and distances between the pieces putting the ⅛" rod between the ³⁄₁₆" rods. (See above.)

STEP EIGHT   On two head pins, put one rondelle and one 8mm bead and form an eye loop.

STEP NINE   Put the 8mm rondelle, the two 6mm rondelles and one 6mm rondelle on the third head pin, then form an eye loop.

STEP TEN   See the photo of the finished piece (right) for the placement of the beaded head pins. Attach them to the rods.

STEP ELEVEN   With hot glue, put the pin back on the back of the finished rectangle.

▶ *Constructed Wood Pin with dangling beads.*

Dyed Turned Wood Earrings & Pin

STEP ONE Cut the basswood to 1½″ × 1″. Lightly sand the edges.

STEP TWO For the pin, cut the turned wood in the following approximate lengths: one piece 1¾″; two pieces 1⅛″; one piece ⅞″; one piece ⅝″; and one piece ¼″. Utilize the pattern of the turned wood when choosing the lengths to cut.

STEP THREE For the earrings, cut two pieces of the turned wood 1¾″ long; two pieces 1⅛″; and two pieces 1⅛″ long.

STEP FOUR Drill one end of each turned piece for the earrings and the smallest piece for the pin.

STEP FIVE Put a drop of white glue on the end of each screw eye. Insert one into each drilled hole.

STEP SIX Dye the flat piece of wood by brushing dye on in stripes, letting the stripes blend together. Set the wood on wax paper to dry.

STEP SEVEN Dye each of the pieces of turned wood for the pin a different color. Use the tweezers to hold the turnings as you brush on or dip the pieces in the dye. Set these on wax paper to dry.

STEP EIGHT For the earring pieces, dye the same length pieces the same color, using three different colors. Allow these to dry on wax paper.

STEP NINE Put one of each of the earring pieces on each ear loop.

STEP TEN Lay out the turned pieces on the rectangle of wood, looking for the best place to tie each piece on. Mark the spots and drill. Also drill a hole within ⅛″ from the bottom edge for a jump ring.

STEP ELEVEN Stitch the pieces onto the rectangle with the button thread and tie off with a knot.

STEP TWELVE Hot-glue the pin back onto the pin.

MATERIALS

⅛″-thick basswood sheet
Small, turned wood pieces from a dollhouse/miniature store
7 ⅛″ screw eyes
Silk dyes—full strength
1 1″ pin back
2 1″ silver ear loops
1 jump ring
Button thread
Cyanoacrylate glue
Wax paper

TOOLS

Drill or Dremel
Jeweler's saw
Sandpaper
Needle-nose pliers
Tweezers
Sewing needle

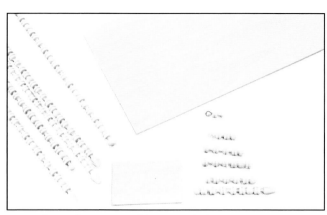

Turned wood pieces and basswood sheet.

Cut, turned pieces for the earrings with screw eyes inserted.

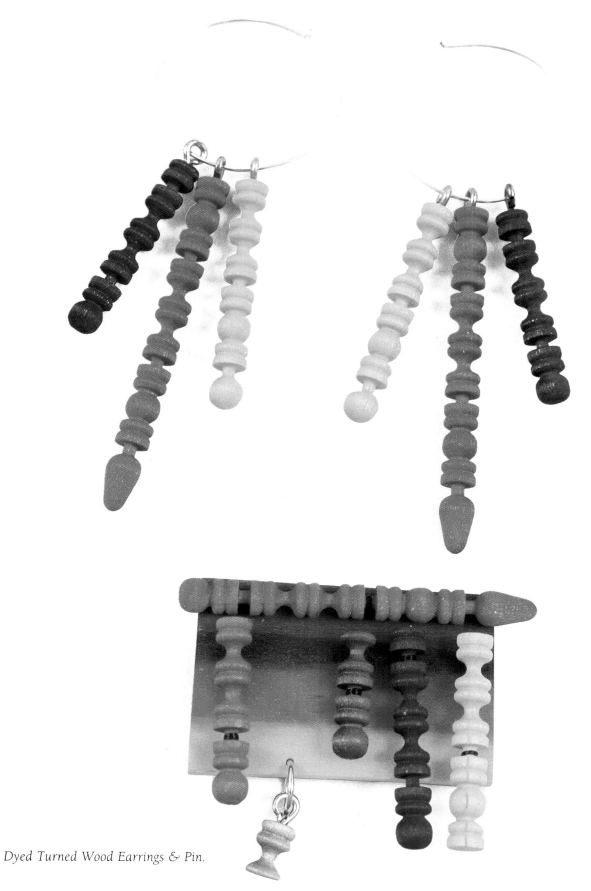

Dyed Turned Wood Earrings & Pin.

Wood Hand Pin & Earrings

STEP ONE   Trace a pair of hands on a piece of paper. Reduce them on a photocopier so you get one set approximately 3½″ × 3″ and one set approximately 1½″ × 1″.

STEP TWO   Draw a cuff shape at the wrist of each of the small hands. On a separate piece of paper, draw a cuff shape for one of the large hands.

STEP THREE   Lay carbon paper on the wood and transfer the drawings of the hands and the large cuff.

STEP FOUR   Cut out all of the pieces. (See photo at right.)

STEP FIVE   Lightly sand all edges of the wood hands.

STEP SIX   Paint the hands with one color and the large cuff with another color. Let these dry.

STEP SEVEN   Sponge-paint three to five layers of paint on both sides of the small hands (which will be your earrings) and one side of the large hand and large cuff (which will be your pin). Refer to page 50 for the painting technique.

STEP EIGHT   Touch up the edges with the background color.

STEP NINE   Glue the large cuff in place on the large hand.

STEP TEN   Hot-glue the pin back on the large hand.

STEP ELEVEN   Drill a hole in the cuff of each small hand.

STEP TWELVE   Add a jump ring and an ear wire to each small hand.

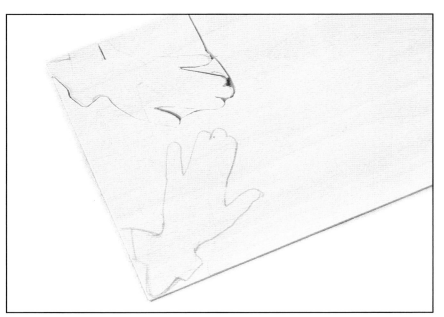

Marking and cutting out hand earring shapes.

MATERIALS

White paper
⅛″-thick basswood sheet
Carbon paper
2   7mm jump rings
2   ear wires
1   1½″ pin back
4 to 5 acrylic paints
Wood glue
Hot glue

TOOLS

Pencil
Jeweler's saw
Drill or Dremel
Sandpaper
Needle-nose pliers
Glue gun
Photocopier
Paint brush
Sponge for painting

▶ *Wood Hand Pin & Earrings.*

Gallery of Paper, Fiber & Wood Jewelry

Photo Credit: C.W. Schauer

Renee Harris, Cincinnati, OH
Way Out
Cotton thread embroidery, niobium coils
1¾" × 1¼" × ⅛"
©1993

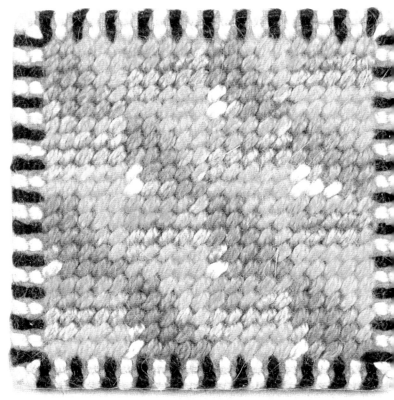

Dianne Dennis, Cincinnati, OH
Needlepoint Pin
Geometric design with black-and-white border
1¾" × 1¾"
©1992

Susan Naylor, Cincinnati, OH
Stripes and Grids
Paper collage
2¼″ × 2¼″
©1994

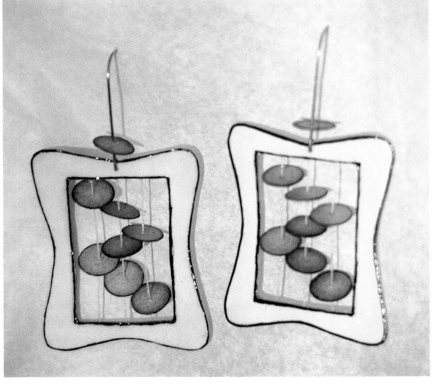

Elizabeth Tait, Woodlawn, OH
Paper Earrings
Paper, colored pencil, watercolor, string
and nail polish
2⅞″ × 1½″ × ⅜″
©1990

Chapter Four

PLASTIC AND RUBBER

I ndustrial materials such as plastic and rubber can be found in the jewelry cases of craft galleries and shops nationwide. However, I have not seen any of these particular projects in those cases.

My favorite project in this section (maybe even in the whole book) is the Black Sheet Rubber Feathered Necklace & Earrings (pages 94-95). I played around with the rubber for quite some time before I came upon this particular solution. When you first see this project, it is hard to tell what it is made of; I find that intriguing.

The sheet vinyl can be purchased at a fabric store; the plastic grid and Fun Foam in crafts supply stores. The plastic disks and sheet rubber I found in a children's museum recycling store, and I bought the rest in a hardware store.

Most of the plastic and rubber in these projects is easy to fold and manipulate. I'm sure you'll discover other inventive projects to create with the materials.

Plastic Confetti Earrings & Pin

STEP ONE Cut the vinyl in half. Stack the two pieces on top of each other, then cut them in half again. Now cut one of these sets in half again.

STEP TWO Draw a 2½″ triangle on the large set, and draw 1½″ triangles on the smaller two sets of vinyl pieces.

STEP THREE Sew two sides of each triangle leaving the threads long at the beginning and end of the stitching.

STEP FOUR Fill the triangles with confetti and stitch closed. Again, leave the threads long.

STEP FIVE Tie knots in the threads and trim the threads so they are approximately 1″ long.

STEP SIX Glue the pin back on the large triangle with the cyanoacrylate glue.

STEP SEVEN Pierce a hole in one corner of each of the smaller triangles. For strength, make sure the holes are inside the stitched area.

STEP EIGHT Add the jump ring and ear wire.

MATERIALS
Clear vinyl sheet approximately 6″ × 12″
Metallic confetti
2 7mm jump rings
2 ear wires
1 1″ pin back
Cyanoacrylate glue

TOOLS
Sewing machine
Needle-nose pliers
T-pin

▶ *Plastic Confetti Earrings & Pin.*

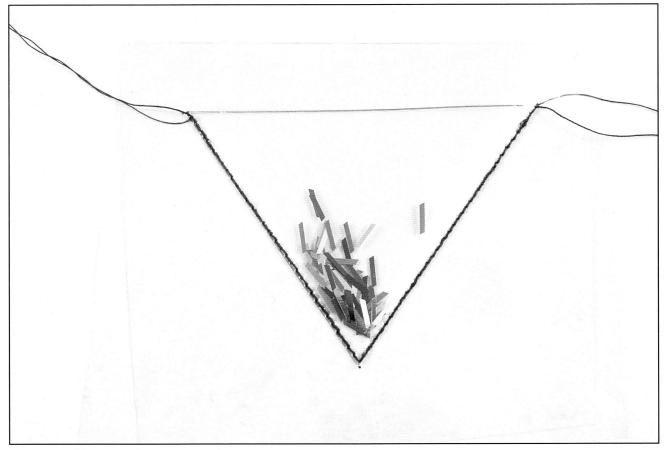

Starting to fill a partially sewn triangle.

Plastic Grid Necklace & Earrings

STEP ONE Cut and layer the plastic canvas in squares of the following sizes. (The number represents the number of little squares within each grid piece.) For the Earrings: Two sets each of four blue, six green and eight red. For the Necklace: Two sets each of three, four, five and six blue and one seven blue; two sets each of four, five, six and seven green and one eight green; two sets each of five, six, seven and eight red and one nine red.

STEP TWO Link each group of three together in a corner with a jump ring.

STEP THREE On the earring sections, add ear wires.

STEP FOUR Take the largest section and string it on to the center of the cord. Tie a knot on either side of the jump ring. (See photo at bottom.)

STEP FIVE Tie a knot 1⅛″ from each knot. Add the next sections and tie knots close to the jump rings.

STEP SIX Repeat the process until all the sections are attached.

STEP SEVEN Trim the ends of the cord so they are each 5½″ from the last knots.

STEP EIGHT Add a crimp to each end. (See technique on page 12.)

STEP NINE Add jump rings on both ends and add the clasp.

Necklace sections held together with jump rings.

MATERIALS

Blue, green and red plastic canvas
13 7mm jump rings
1   clasp
2   crimps
30″ of red satin cord

TOOLS

Scissors that can cut through thick plastic
T-pin
Needle-nose pliers

Controlling the location of the second knot with a pin.

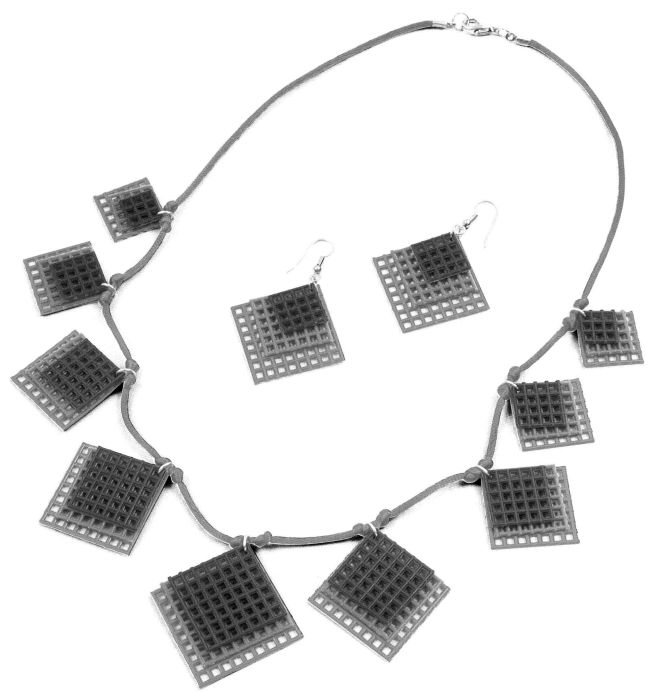

Plastic Grid Necklace & Earrings.

Cut-Out Plastic Laminate Earrings & Pin

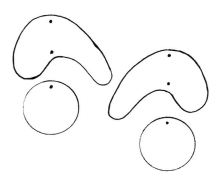

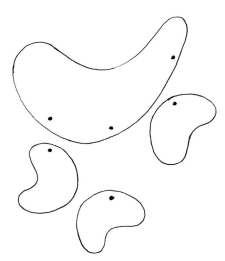

Patterns for the earrings and pin.

STEP ONE Using carbon paper, trace the pattern shapes on this page onto a clean piece of card stock. Cut out and trace shapes with a pencil onto the laminate. (See patterns for the sizes.)

STEP TWO With a jeweler's saw, cut out the shapes. Don't forget to use beeswax on the blade.

STEP THREE Drill holes at the locations shown on the patterns.

STEP FOUR Sand the edges.

STEP FIVE Put a jump ring in each hole of the odd-shaped earring pieces. In the top ring add an ear wire; in the bottom ring attach a disk.

STEP SIX In the large piece, attach the smaller shapes using three jump rings each. (See the photo of the finished piece for colored shape placement.)

STEP SEVEN Attach the pin back with cyanoacrylate glue.

Layout of cut pieces before drilling.

MATERIALS

Red, purple, green and yellow
    plastic laminate scraps
13 7mm jump rings
1   1″ pin back
2   ear wires
Carbon paper
Piece of card stock
Cyanoacrylate glue
Beeswax

TOOLS

Pencil
Jeweler's saw
Sandpaper
Drill or Dremel
Needle-nose pliers
Scissors

Plastic Laminate Earrings & Pin made from countertop scraps and samples.

Recycled Plastic Disks With Dangling Beads

STEP ONE   Hot-glue disks in an overlapping arrangement.

STEP TWO   Drill three holes in the bottom disk. Place them off center and put ½″ between the first and second hole and ¼″ between the second and third holes. They should be ¹⁄₁₆″ from the edge of the disk.

STEP THREE   On one head pin, stack the 10mm pink cylinder bead, 8mm round purple bead and the 10mm long-shaped turquoise bead. Form an eye loop. Attach this to the left hole with a jump ring.

STEP FOUR   On a head pin stack the 4mm round purple bead and the 10mm round red bead. Form an eye loop. On another head pin stack the 8mm round yellow bead and the 8mm red rondelle. Form an eye loop.

STEP FIVE   Put the 8mm green rondelle on a head pin and put it through the middle hole. Bend it down in the back and add the light blue cylinder bead. Form the eye loop so the bead hangs below the disk. Attach the yellow and red beaded head pin.

STEP SIX   Put a 6mm red rondelle on a head pin. Put it through the right hole, bend it down in back, and add the four cobalt beads. Make an eye loop and attach the red and purple beaded head pin.

STEP SEVEN   Attach the pin back with hot glue.

MATERIALS

3	1½″ plastic disks
1	10mm pink cylinder bead
1	8mm round purple bead
1	10mm long-shaped turquoise bead
1	8mm green rondelle
1	10mm light blue cylinder bead
1	8mm round yellow bead
1	8mm red rondelle
1	6mm red rondelle
4	6mm round cobalt beads
1	4mm round purple bead
1	10mm round red bead
5	head pins
1	7mm jump ring
1	1″ pin back

Hot glue

TOOLS

Drill or Dremel
Round-nose pliers
Needle-nose pliers
Glue gun

▶ *Recycled Plastic Disks With Dangling Beads.*

Friendly Plastic Pins & Earrings

Baking cut shapes onto sheets of Friendly Plastic.

STEP ONE   Choose four sheets of the patterned Friendly Plastic. Place them on a cookie sheet covered with aluminum foil.

STEP TWO   Cut a variety of small shapes (such as triangles and squares) out of the three solid colors. Limit their size to about 1/4".

STEP THREE   Lay the cut pieces close together on top of the Friendly Plastic sheets on the cookie sheet (see above).

STEP FOUR   Bake these in a 350°F oven for four minutes—just enough time to fuse the pieces together. Let them cool and then peel the sheets off the foil.

STEP FIVE   Cut the sheets in half the short way to make two square pieces.

STEP SIX   Heat the water in the electric frying pan (or on the stove) to between 150°F and 200°F. Using the tongue depressor, place one piece of Friendly Plastic in the hot water until it begins to sag on the stick. Remove it from the water. With your hands (be careful, it will be quite warm), roll it gently into a ball, cylinder or tube. Drop it into a glass of ice water and allow it to cool.

Beads and formed shapes of Friendly Plastic.

STEP SEVEN Repeat the process for all of the bead shapes.

STEP EIGHT For the bar of the bar pins, take one piece of the patterned Friendly Plastic and soften it in the water as in Step Six. When you remove it from the water, gently roll it into a cylinder and flatten it. Set it on a flat surface to cool.

STEP NINE To make a flat disk for a pin, take either a whole piece or a half piece of Friendly Plastic and soften in hot water as described in Step Six. When you remove it from the water, gently roll it into a ball and then flatten it. Set it on a flat surface to cool.

STEP TEN Drill a hole through each bead. Don't run the drill too long at any one time or it will melt the Friendly Plastic.

STEP ELEVEN Drill two holes up into the bottom edge of the bar pins, deep enough to set the eye hooks. Use cyanoacrylate glue to put the hooks in place.

STEP TWELVE For the disk pins, drill a hole in the front within ¼″ of the edge.

STEP THIRTEEN Stack the Friendly Plastic beads on the head pins with glass beads. Form eye loops and attach these to the pin bases or ear wires.

STEP FOURTEEN Use hot glue to attach the pin backs.

MATERIALS

6 different patterned pieces of Friendly Plastic
3 different solid-colored pieces of Friendly Plastic
Ice water
Ear wires
Pin backs
A variety of glass beads
Aluminum foil
Cyanoacrylate glue
Hot glue
⅛″ eye hooks (2 for each bar pin)

TOOLS

Cookie sheet
Strong pair of scissors or tin snips
Oven—regular or toaster
Electric frying pan with water or deep frying pan with water
Stove
Popsicle stick or tongue depressor
Drill or Dremel
Glue gun

Friendly Plastic Pins & Earrings embellished with glass beads.

Plastic Tube Necklace & Bracelet With Seed Beads

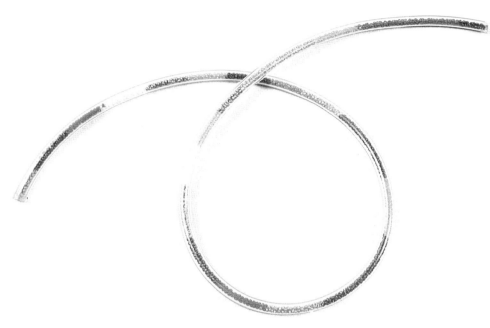

◀ *Filling a ⁵⁄₁₆″ diameter clear vinyl tube with seed beads.*

TO MAKE THE NECKLACE:

STEP ONE Cut a 1″ length of each tubing. Set these aside.

STEP TWO Tape off the end of the large tube to keep the beads from falling out.

STEP THREE Determine the order in which you wish to have the colored beads.

STEP FOUR Fill ¾″ to ⅞″ of the tube with the first color, then continue with each color. Once you have put each color in the tube, continue to repeat the order until the tube is nearly full.

STEP FIVE Put the 1″ piece of ³⁄₁₆″ tubing halfway into the open end of the mostly full necklace tube. Fill the connector tube with beads, remove the tape and insert the connector section into the other end of the long tube.

TO MAKE THE BRACELET:

STEP ONE Tape one end of the ³⁄₁₆″ tube and fill it in the same order as the necklace using five beads of each color at a time.

STEP TWO Place the 1″ length of the ⁵⁄₁₆″ tubing on the outside of the open end. Remove the tape and place the end inside the connector.

Note: *If the tubes are not sliding together easily, you can lightly wet them to help. You may also wish to put a bit of cyanoacrylate glue around the joints to make them a bit more secure.*

Plastic Tube Necklace & Bracelet
filled with glass seed beads.

Fun Foam Earrings & Pin

TO MAKE THE EARRINGS:

STEP ONE With the straight pin, put a hole in the centers of two blue disks, two black disks and two yellow ovals.

STEP TWO Gently fold the two purple disks in half (be careful not to crease them). Put holes through the two ends, centered and ³⁄₁₆″ from the edge.

STEP THREE On a head pin, first place a yellow disk, one end of the purple oval, a black disk, a blue disk, and the other end of the oval disk. (See below.)

STEP FOUR With the needle-nose pliers, gently fold the head pin 90°. At the end of the head pin form an eye loop and attach it to an ear wire.

STEP FIVE Repeat Steps Three and Four for the other earring.

TO MAKE THE PIN:

STEP ONE Fold a purple disk and wrap it around the edge of a blue disk. Stitch them together. Take the second purple disk and do the same on the opposite side of the blue disk.

STEP TWO Stack the black disk on top of a yellow oval and place it on the center of the blue disk (with the purple sewn to it). Stitch these together.

STEP THREE Use the hot glue to put the pin back in place.

Note: *Be careful not to pull the threads too tight as the Fun Foam will tear easily.*

MATERIALS

Fun Foam shapes:
- 2 large purple ovals
- 2 large purple circles
- 3 small yellow ovals
- 3 medium blue disks
- 3 small black disks

2	2″ head pins
2	ear wires
1	1½″ pin back

Black button thread
Hot glue

TOOLS

Straight pin
Sewing needle
Needle-nose pliers
Round-nose pliers
Glue gun

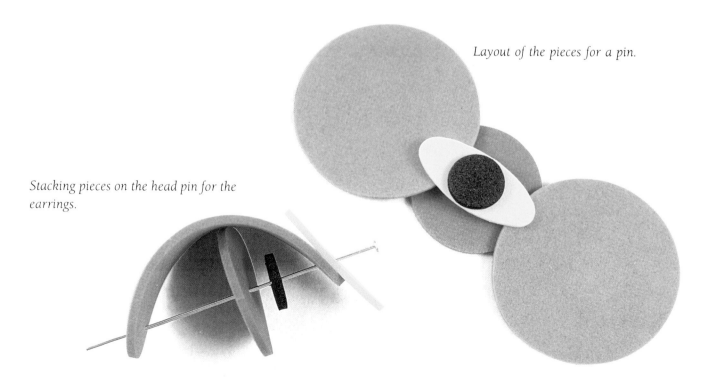

Layout of the pieces for a pin.

Stacking pieces on the head pin for the earrings.

Folded Fun Foam shapes make a great pair of earrings and a pin.

Rubber O-Ring Gasket Bracelet

STEP ONE Construct the center section by placing a 1" O-ring inside a 1⅜" O-ring. Then place both rings sideways inside a 1" O-ring. Squeeze the outermost 1" ring together and bind it with a 10mm jump ring as shown in the first photo.

STEP TWO Lock two 1⅛" O-rings together as shown in the second photo. Do the same with a second pair of O-rings.

STEP THREE Lay out all sections as shown in the final piece. Join them together with 10mm jump rings.

STEP FOUR Attach the 7mm jump rings to the last two O-rings and attach the lobster claw clasp to one side.

Putting the center section together.

MATERIALS	
1	1 ⅜" O.D. O-ring
4	1" O.D. O-rings
4	1⅛" O.D. O-rings
5	10mm jump rings
2	7mm jump rings
1	lobster claw clasp

TOOLS

Needle-nose pliers (two pairs if available)

Interlocking two O-rings together.

▶ *Rubber O-Ring Gasket Bracelet fastened and laid flat to show all the parts.*

Stacked Colorful Rubber Tubing Necklace & Earrings

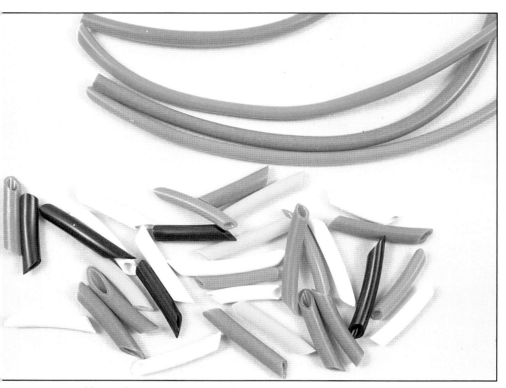

Rubber tubing cut to various lengths.

MATERIALS

2' lengths of ¼" colored tubing in the following colors: black, white, orange, green, blue, yellow and hot pink
36" of tiger tail (a finely woven cable with a plastic coating)
4   crimp beads
2   split rings
1   jump ring
2   head pins
2   ear wires

TOOLS

Scissors
Needle-nose pliers
Round-nose pliers
Large-hole needle for tiger tail
Masking or cellophane tape

TO MAKE THE EARRINGS:

STEP ONE Cut eight black pieces of rubber tubing in lengths varying from ⅞" to 1⅛" long. Cut one each of the other colors, also varying the lengths. Cut them so the ends are angled in different directions. (See above.)

STEP TWO On one head pin, alternate the black pieces with green, orange and white. On the other head pin alternate black with blue, pink and yellow.

STEP THREE Form eye loops and attach these to ear wires.

TO MAKE THE NECKLACE:

STEP ONE Cut twenty-seven pieces of each color plus one extra black piece. Vary the lengths between ⅞" to 1¾". Cut them so the ends are angled in different directions.

STEP TWO Thread one end of the tiger tail into the needle. Place a piece of tape on the other end of the tiger tail.

STEP THREE Poke a hole in the center of each piece of rubber as you thread it onto the tiger tail. Place a black piece on first, then one of each of the other colors, then another black piece. Repeat, placing one of each color in random order between the black pieces. When all of the colors have been used, finish off with a black piece.

STEP FOUR Attach split rings on both ends using the crimp beads. (See the technique on page 11.)

STEP FIVE Add the clasp to one split ring.

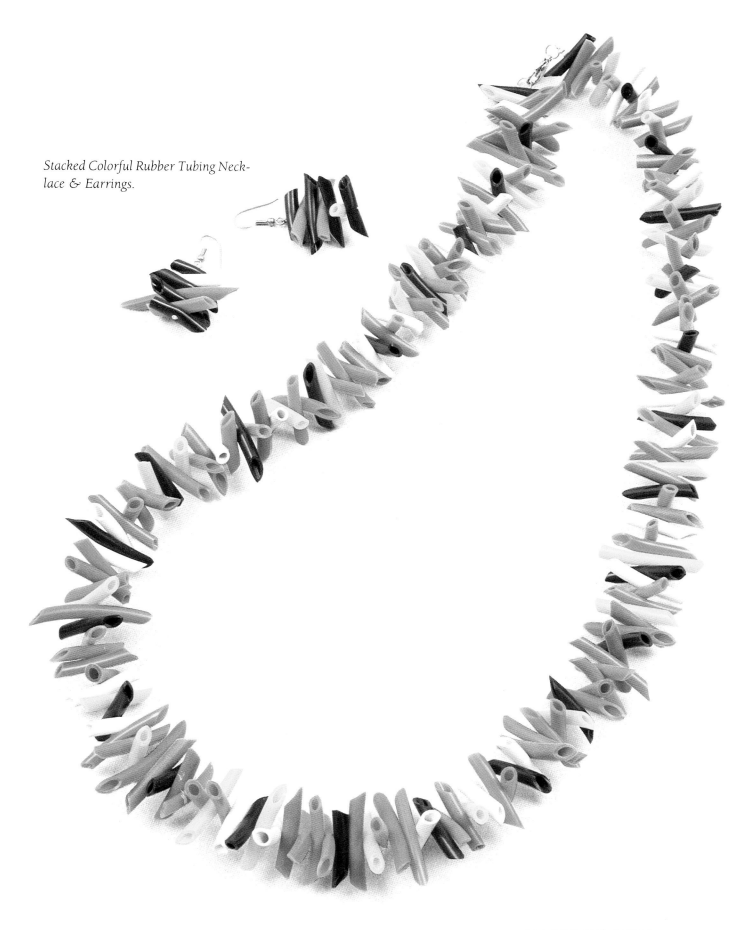

Stacked Colorful Rubber Tubing Necklace & Earrings.

Black Sheet Rubber Feathered Necklace & Earrings

Process of stringing rubber triangles.

MATERIALS
28″ clear vinyl tubing (³⁄₁₆″ in diameter)
1′ to 2′ square thin rubber sheet
2 crimps
1 large barrel clasp
2 10mm jump rings
2 ear wires

MATERIALS

28″ clear vinyl tubing ($^3/_{16}$″ in
  diameter)
1′ to 2′ square thin rubber sheet
2　crimps
1　large barrel clasp
2　10mm jump rings
2　ear wires

TOOLS

Scissors
T-pin
Ruler
Needle-nose pliers

TO MAKE THE NECKLACE:

STEP ONE Cut seventy black rubber triangles. Cut them all 2″ across the top and vary lengths from 2″ long to 3$^1/_4$″ long.

STEP TWO Cut both ends of the tubing at a sharp diagonal.

STEP THREE Fold each triangle in half and pierce with the T-pin $^1/_4$″ down from the top and centered on each side of the fold. Then thread them onto the tubing. (See above.) As you thread them on and set them in place, separate the fold $^1/_4$″.

STEP FOUR Alternate shorter triangles between longer triangles. Pull the tips of the shorter ones forward.

STEP FIVE Trim the tubing to the length you want, and attach crimps. (See technique on page 12.)

STEP SIX Attach the barrel clasp.

TO MAKE THE EARRINGS:

STEP ONE Cut six triangles measuring 1$^1/_2$″ across the top and varying from 2″ to 2$^1/_2$″ long. You may consider cutting two each of three different lengths.

STEP TWO Fold the triangles in half and pierce them $^3/_{16}$″ down from the top and centered on each side of the fold.

STEP THREE Place three triangles on each jump ring. The center one faces the opposite direction.

STEP FOUR Attach these to the ear wire so the two outer triangles will be curved-side-out.

Note: *Fun Foam can also be used in this project. However, it will be a bit stiffer.*

The back of the necklace.

Black Sheet Rubber Feathered Neck-
lace & Earrings.

Gallery of Plastic & Rubber Jewelry

Carol Grape
Red Finger Necklace
Rubber, glass beads
21½" long
© 1995

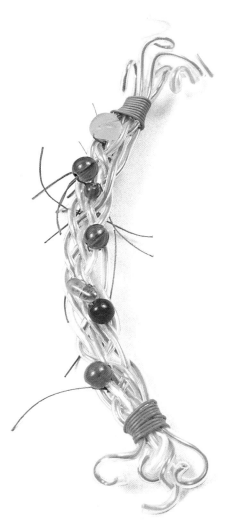

Carol Grape
Braided Squiggle Pin
Vinyl tubing, phone wire, glass beads, thread
5¼" × 1" × ¾"
© 1995

Nancy Kunkle Thompson, Richmond, VA
Brooch
Hard rubber, copper, green patina
6" × 1" × ¾"
©1993

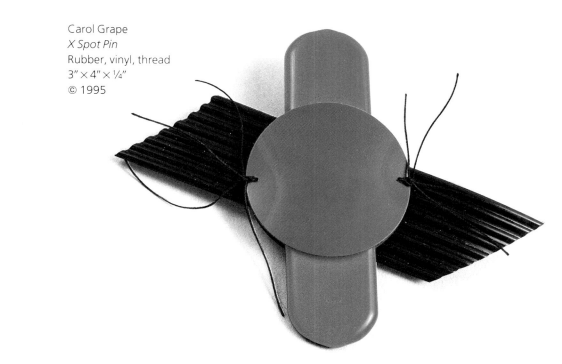

Carol Grape
X Spot Pin
Rubber, vinyl, thread
3″ × 4″ × ¼″
© 1995

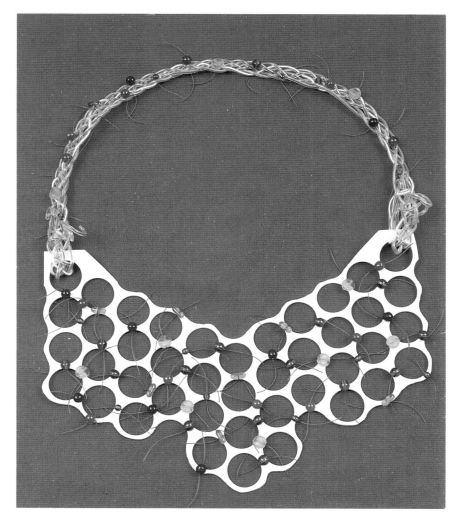

Carol Grape
42-50 Necklace
Rubber, glass beads, vinyl tubing, phone
wire, thread
11″ × 9″ × ¾″
© 1995

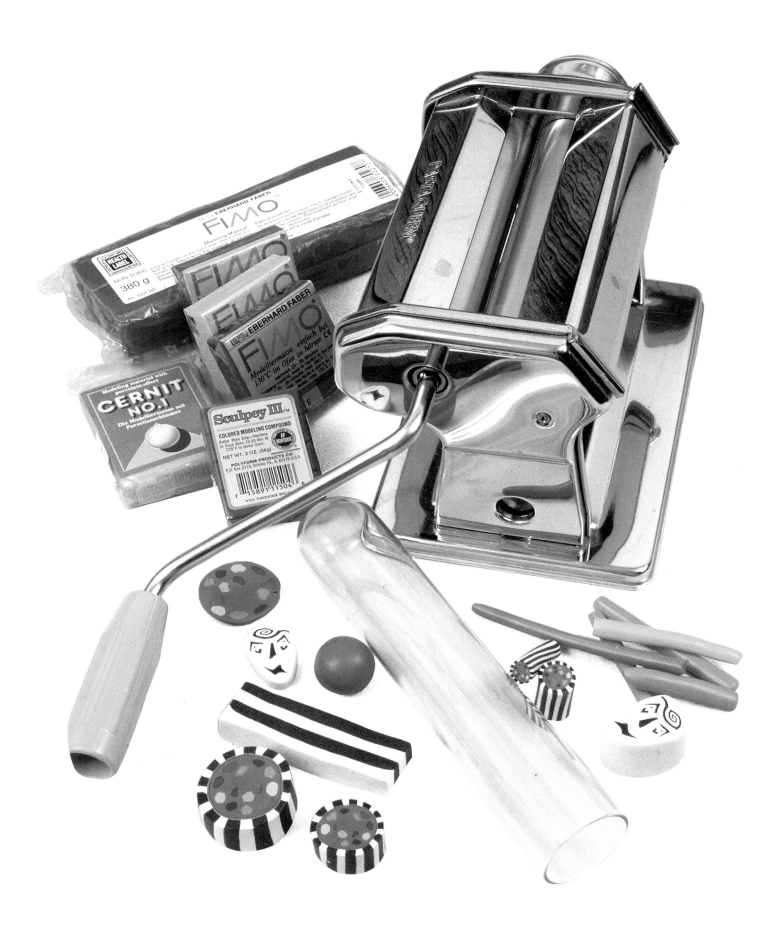

Chapter Five

POLYMER CLAYS

Polymer clay is an exciting medium for jewelry. It has been around for thirty-plus years but has really only been used for jewelry in the past ten to fifteen years. Unlike ceramic clay, polymer clay takes very little equipment, requires no glazing, and doesn't shrink or change shape in the curing process. It also comes in great colors.

There are a variety of polymer clays on the market—FIMO is the stiffest and comes in wonderful colors. Sculpey III is the softest and though the color selection has gotten better, in my opinion, the choices aren't as good as they are with FIMO. Cernit has a more porcelain look. And because these clays are all made of polyvinyl chloride they can all be mixed together.

One way to choose colors is to look at your environment. We all tend to gravitate toward a few favorite colors—start with those.

You can create your own colors by mixing together the manufactured colors. You may even consider mixing the stiffer FIMO with the softer Sculpey III to create a more workable clay. I personally have used FIMO the most because it creates a cleaner, crisper pattern. The softer the clay, the more apt the color is to run together, which can be of great benefit if you are creating a marbleized effect.

The curing process will darken most of the colors slightly. If you are going to create a polymer clay cane using fairly dark colors, it is a good idea to choose at least one lighter color to use between the dark colors. It is hard to see the difference in the dark colors when they are next to each other once they are cured. However, the lighter colors hold their own even if they are close in value.

When making these projects it is easiest to make all of your polymer clay components first, bake them all together (following the directions on the package) and then assemble them. You will have some cane left over from these projects—have fun.

How to Handle Polymer Clay

SAFETY TIPS

Even though these packages of polymer clay are marked non-toxic, you must take precautions when using this material. Make sure you wash your hands well after use. Use a nylon scrubber to get the clay out of your pores without damaging your skin.

If you are just doing a few projects, you can use your oven, but completely air it out before cooking food again. Or, you may wish to create your own solar oven. Polymer clay will cure in a plastic container in a hot car. It will probably take a bit longer to cure the clay, but it may be easier on you. If you are planning on working with polymer clays on a regular basis, consider investing in a new toaster oven with a thermostatic control. I would also recommend placing the oven either in your garage or near an open window.

This is a fun medium for kids, but make sure they don't ingest any and wash their hands thoroughly when finished.

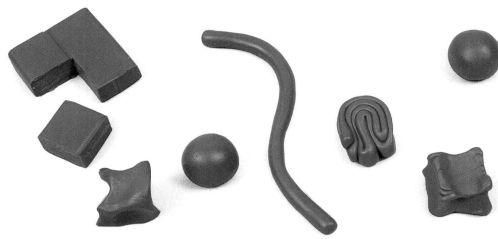

Preparing FIMO.

HOW TO PREPARE FIMO

If you have tried FIMO and found it difficult to work with, try the following technique. I learned it in a class from Jamey D. Allen, a prominent polymer clay artist. It keeps the FIMO from crumbling and the air bubbles to a minimum. Wash your hands before starting and in between working with each color, as there will be some residue. Knead your lightest colors first.

If you are going to be seriously producing a lot of FIMO items, you may wish to invest in a food processor to knead FIMO and mix colors. It is much faster and easier on your arms and hands. A pasta machine is great for kneading and mixing Sculpey III and rolling thin, even layers of all polymer clays. FIMO does need to be rolled out before placing it in the pasta machine as the clay will crack if forced through when thick.

KNEADING FIMO BY HAND

STEP ONE Cut the block into quarters.

STEP TWO Gently start squashing the cube, rotating it to soften it from all sides until the sides become concave.

STEP THREE Roll it into a ball.

STEP FOUR Roll it out into a log approximately 8″ long.

STEP FIVE Fold the FIMO in half, squeezing it from the fold out.

STEP SIX Fold it in half two more times.

STEP SEVEN Squash it into a cube.

STEP EIGHT Roll it into a ball and set it aside.

Note: *If the FIMO cracks at any time during the process repeat Steps Two through Eight.*

FIMO Earrings, Pin, Necklace & Barrette

STEP ONE Knead all the FIMO, as shown on page 100, ¼ block at a time.

CREATING THE SPIRAL

STEP ONE Start by stacking one ¼-block ball of Green and one ¼-block ball of Magenta, then gently press them together applying even pressure.

STEP TWO Begin to form the two

Creating a spiral cane.

balls into a square, flattening the sides as you work.

STEP THREE Begin stretching and squeezing in one direction to form an elongated rectangle. Continue to keep all sides as straight as possible.

STEP FOUR Once the elongated rectangle is fairly thin, lay it on a clean surface and trim each end.

STEP FIVE Gently roll it into a spiral and set it aside.

CREATING STRIPES

STEP ONE Start by stacking one ¼-block ball of Violet and one ¼-block ball of Yellow and gently press them together applying even pressure.

STEP TWO As you are doing this, begin to form this into a square flattening the sides as you work (just as you began the spiral).

STEP THREE Begin stretching and squeezing in one direction to form an elongated rectangle. Keep all sides as straight as possible. Keep one side the same length as the spiral log.

STEP FOUR Once the rectangle is twice as long as the spiral in one

Completing the cane with stripes.

direction, cut it in half and stack Violet to Yellow, making sure the two halves are attached.

STEP FIVE Stand the clay upright and trim it off to make one smooth edge. Then cut six slices each approximately ⅛″ thick.

FINISHING THE CANE

STEP ONE Gently place the stripes on the outside of the spiral until you cover it all the way around.

STEP TWO Gently squeeze the sides to blend the seams together.

STEP THREE Roll on a smooth surface until the cane is approximately 1″ in diameter.

Note: *As you roll the cane, the excess will push to the ends, collapse a bit and become concave. When you cut off the ends you can save them for the future.*

STEP FOUR Cut the cane in half and set half aside. Roll the other half until it's approximately ¾″ in diameter. Slice it in half again.

STEP FIVE Continue this process, cutting at ½″ diameter and ¼″ diameter.

A variety of cane sizes showing the pattern is visible no matter how small.

CONSTRUCTING THE PIECES

The Earrings

STEP ONE Cut two ¼"-long slices of 1" thick cane and pierce them with a T-pin through the center of the ¼" edge.

Note: *Rotate the cane after each cut for less distortion and, after slicing, gently reshape the slice into a circle with your fingers.*

STEP TWO Place each slice on a separate T-pin to bake.

The Pin

STEP ONE Knead ⅛ block of Violet and roll it into a ball.

STEP TWO Place a variety of slices mostly on one-half of the ball's surface.

STEP THREE Roll the ball in your hand to incorporate the slices into the surface.

STEP FOUR Flatten the ball into a disk until it's approximately 1½" in diameter and slightly less than ¼" thick.

STEP FIVE Place the clay flat on a tray to bake.

The Barrette

STEP ONE Slice approximately a ⁵⁄₁₆"-thick piece of the Yellow-and-Purple striped block.

STEP TWO Gently stretch it to cover the 2¾"-long barrette clip.

STEP THREE Place a variety of slices on the surface and blend in as desired.

STEP FOUR Bake this on the barrette clip. This way, the clay will form to the shape of the clip and will be less likely to fall off once glued.

The Necklace

For this necklace make thirteen FIMO beads in a variety of sizes and a couple of shapes.

STEP ONE Start by kneading a few pieces of solid color: ⅛ block of Violet, ¼ block of Green and ¼ block of Magenta.

STEP TWO The ¼ blocks of Green and Magenta can be cut into three or four pieces and a variety of slices can be added to each one. Keep the Violet piece whole and add slices—use it as the center bead.

STEP THREE Use the leftover Purple-and-Yellow stripe to create cylinder-shaped beads.

STEP FOUR Use up the scraps and apply a variety of slices on them to create unique beads. You may wish to use a big slice as a bead.

STEP FIVE Place all of the beads on T-pins and bake.

FIMO parts ready to cure. Start with a cold oven, set it to 265°F, and bake for thirty-five minutes.

FINISHING THE JEWELRY

The pin and the barrette should be glued to their findings with cyanoacrylate glue.

Finishing the Earrings With Glass Beads

STEP ONE On a head pin, place a green rondelle, the FIMO bead, a purple bead, and a yellow rondelle.

MATERIALS	
4	4mm round purple beads
2	6mm yellow rondelles
2	6 mm green rondelles
2	2" head pins
2	sterling silver French ear wires

STEP TWO Fold down the head pin, cut it at ⅜" and form a loop.

STEP THREE Place the purple bead on an ear wire and form a loop.

STEP FOUR Attach the head pin to the ear wire.

Finishing the Necklace With Glass Beads

STEP ONE On a towel lay out FIMO beads with the variety of glass beads listed. See the order shown in the finished necklace.

STEP TWO String the beads on a tiger tail.

STEP THREE Attach a spring ring to one end using a crimp bead. See the technique on page 11.

STEP FOUR Attach a split ring on the other end with a crimp bead. Pull these tight and crimp.

MATERIALS	
8	6mm round green beads
6	6mm round red beads
10	6mm round purple beads
6	6mm round yellow beads
2	8mm round purple beads
2	7.5mm shaped yellow beads
6	6mm green rondelles
10	6mm red rondelles
2	6mm yellow rondelles
4	8mm yellow rondelles
2	8mm green rondelles
10	10mm red cylinder beads
7	10mm green cylinder beads
1	6mm green cylinder bead
Tiger tail	
2	Spring rings
Split ring	
2	crimp beads

FIMO Earrings, Pin, Necklace & Barrette.

Sculpey III Striped Spiral Buttons

STEP ONE Make a striped block of Sculpey III with a ⅛ block each of Ivory Brilliant, Brown, Copper, Bronze and Green. (See Creating Stripes, page 101.)

STEP TWO Mix ⅛ block of Purple Brilliant with ⅛ block of Ivory Brilliant and roll it out to approximately 1/16″ thick and the width of the striped roll.

STEP THREE Place the stripes side by side on the Purple slab. Trim the Purple to size. Turn the clay over.

STEP FOUR Roll ⅛ block of Green into a log and place it at the end of the slab.

STEP FIVE Gently roll around the Green log. (See below.)

STEP SIX Roll the cane to the desired size of the buttons. Refrigerate for one plus hours.

STEP SEVEN Remove the clay from the refrigerator and slice ⅛″-thick disks.

STEP EIGHT Pierce the disks with a T-pin, then enlarge the holes with a bigger needle.

STEP NINE Lay the disks on a pan and bake.

MATERIALS

Sculpey III in the following colors and quantities:

¼ block #501 Ivory Brilliant
⅛ block #052 Brown
⅛ block #1017 Copper
⅛ block #1085 Bronze
¼ block #022 Green
⅛ block # 512 Purple Brilliant

TOOLS

Knife
Roller
T-pin
A fat needle

Polymer clay buttons should not be dry-cleaned, as the chemicals used in the process can damage the clay. Polymer clay buttons are more easily broken than regular plastic buttons, but don't let that discourage you from trying to make them. I have washed and dried a cotton sweater with FIMO buttons in machines and in three years lost only one button.

Another way to use polymer clay buttons is with button covers. Cut the disks and bake them. Lightly sand the top of a metal button cover, put on a few drops of cyano-acrylate glue, place the polymer clay disk on top and let it dry.

Rolling stripes around a center core.

Sculpey III Striped Spiral Buttons.

Sculpey III Herringbone Pattern Pins & Coiled Earrings

THE HERRINGBONE PATTERN

STEP ONE Roll out each piece of Sculpey III until it is approximately ¼″ in diameter.

STEP TWO Stack the four colors and gently roll them together until they are bonded. (See first photo.)

STEP THREE Cut the clay in half. Twist one half clockwise as you roll it. Continue rolling until it is approximately ¼″ in diameter.

STEP FOUR Take the other half and twist it counterclockwise and roll it to the same size as the first piece. (See first photo.)

STEP FIVE Trim the ends of each roll. Cut three pieces 1½″ long from each.

STEP SIX Lay the sections side by side, alternating from each roll. (See above, right.)

STEP SEVEN Gently squish the sides together so the sections stick to one another. If you want a flatter look you can roll it with a non-porous roller.

STEP EIGHT Trim the ends of the rectangle. Add a twisted piece of clay to each end, and trim.

STEP NINE At this point you can shape the rectangle. (See photo at right.)

FORMING THE COIL

STEP TEN Using the excess twisted pieces, gently roll the ends and form an elongated cone. Keep the large end ¼″ in diameter. (See photo below.)

STEP ELEVEN Roll the cone clockwise into a coil approximately 1″ across at the widest point. Trim the end flat. (See photo below.)

STEP TWELVE Repeat Step Eleven, rolling in a counterclockwise direction.

STEP THIRTEEN Cure all the pieces flat on the baking sheet.

STEP FOURTEEN Attach pin backs and earring posts with cyanoacrylate glue.

▼ *On the left: One straight herringbone pattern and one shaped with a coil attached. On the right: Creating twisted coils.*

Steps for creating the herringbone pattern.

MATERIALS
⅛ block Sculpey III of each:
#501 Ivory Brilliant
#052 Brown
#1017 Copper
#1085 Bronze
2   1½″ pin backs
2   earring posts
2   ear nuts
Cyanoacrylate glue
TOOLS
Knife
Oven

Sculpey III Herringbone Pattern Pins & Coiled Earrings.

Fun FIMO Face Pins & Earrings

STEP ONE Knead a ¹/₁₆ block of each color and roll each block out to approximately 6″ long.

STEP TWO Stack the Yellow, Red and Turquoise together into a triangle. Twist these clockwise, and at the same time roll them together until the log is approximately ¼″ in diameter.

STEP THREE Repeat Step Two with Violet, Pink and Green.

STEP FOUR Cut the logs in half and stack them together, alternating the colors. Then continue twisting the clay clockwise while rolling it. Roll until they are ¼″ to ½″ in diameter.

STEP FIVE Knead the rest of the Red, Violet and Turquoise.

STEP SIX For pins, use ¹/₁₆ block of a solid color for the face. For the earrings, cut that in half. Roll each piece into a ball.

STEP SEVEN To finish the face, roll the solid ball out until it is the thickness of the striped log. Wrap the striped log three-quarters of the way around the flattened ball and trim the ends of the "hair" at an upward angle.

STEP EIGHT Continue rolling the face flat until it is approximately ¹/₈″ thick.

STEP NINE Take a few small scraps of the striped log and roll them out, continuing to twist, until it is approximately ¹/₁₆″ thick. Cut the clay into three pieces ³/₈″ to ½″ long. Taper the ends.

STEP TEN Place the pieces from Step Nine on the face to form bangs.

STEP ELEVEN For the eyes, make two ¹/₈″ balls of the Night Glow. Slightly flatten these and place them on the face.

STEP TWELVE Take a speck of Black and place it on each eye ball. Consider having the eyes looking in a particular direction.

STEP THIRTEEN Roll out the Night Glow to ¹/₁₆″ thick, and cut out nose shapes and place on the face.

STEP FOURTEEN Roll out logs of

STEP FIFTEEN Gently roll all the forms on the face so they attach well to the base but do not distort.

STEP SIXTEEN Bake flat. When cool, drill holes in the small heads. Attach jump rings and ear wires.

STEP SEVENTEEN Attach pin backs on the large heads with cyanoacrylate glue.

Night Glow ¹/₁₆″ in diameter and cut them to ½″ long. Tapering the ends, form a mouth and put it in place.

MATERIALS

FIMO in the following quantities and colors:

- ³/₁₆ block #2 Red
- ³/₁₆ block #6 Violet
- ¹/₁₆ block #5 Green
- ¹/₁₆ block #15 Golden Yellow
- ³/₁₆ block #32 Light Turquoise
- ¹/₁₆ block #20 Pink
- 1 very small piece of #9 Black
- ¹/₁₆ block of #04 Night Glow (glows in the dark)
- 2 jump rings
- 2 ear wires
- 5 1″ pin backs
- Cyanoacrylate glue

TOOLS

Nonporous roller
Drill or Dremel
Needle-nose pliers
Knife

Steps to making fun faces.

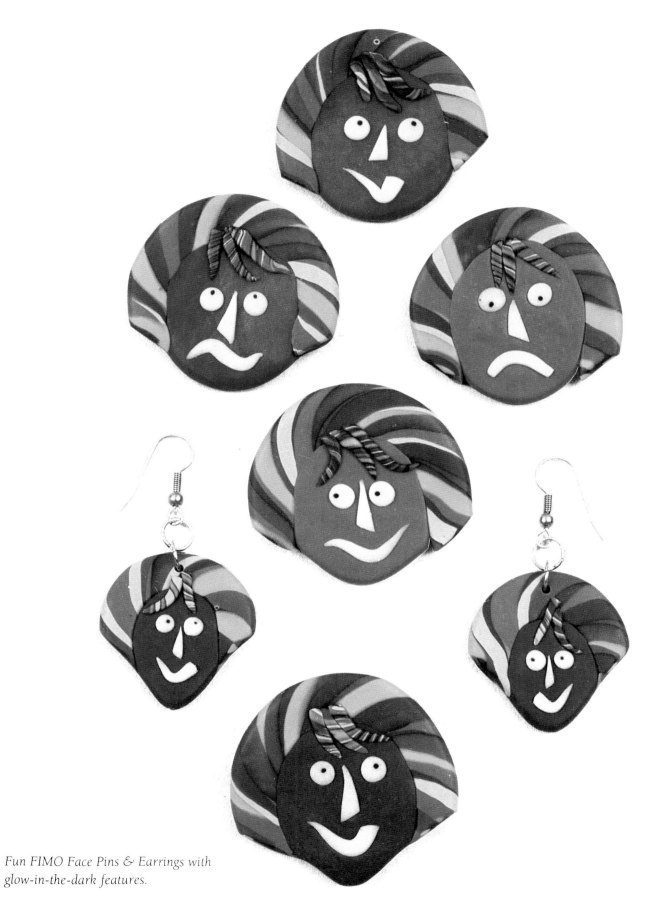

Fun FIMO Face Pins & Earrings with glow-in-the-dark features.

Marbled Bead Necklace, Earrings & Bracelet

STEP ONE   Knead all the colors you have chosen and roll them out into 8″-long logs.

STEP TWO   Stack groups of two to three colors together. Roll each stack together, twisting as you roll.

STEP THREE   When they are doubled in length, cut them in half and set aside until all colors are done.

STEP FOUR   Stack all the rolled logs from Step Three together and roll the clay out again.

STEP FIVE   Fold the clay in half three times and roll it into a ball. If this is not marbleized enough for you, repeat Steps Four and Five.

STEP SIX   Cut the ball in half. Set half aside and roll the other into a log approximately ¾″ in diameter.

STEP SEVEN   For the earrings, cut four pieces of the log approximately ½″ thick.

STEP EIGHT   Roll the four pieces from Step Seven into balls and slightly flatten two of the balls.

STEP NINE   Pierce all four balls with T-pins and then place them on a baking sheet.

STEP TEN   For the bracelet, cut seven ⅜″-thick pieces from the log you made in Step Six.

STEP ELEVEN   Roll four balls, one cylinder and one square. Leave one a disk.

STEP TWELVE   Put these on T-pins and place on a baking sheet.

STEP THIRTEEN   For the necklace, take the half ball you set aside in Step Six and cut off a piece that is about one-sixth of it.

STEP FOURTEEN   Roll the small piece into a ball and flatten it until it is approximately ¼″ thick. Pierce this piece with a T-pin and place it on the baking sheet.

STEP FIFTEEN   Roll the large piece into a ball and, with your palms, gently flatten it until the sides are thinner than the center.

STEP SIXTEEN   Place the large bead on the knitting needle to bake.

STEP SEVENTEEN   Cure all the pieces in the oven.

STEP EIGHTEEN   For the earrings, put the FIMO disks each on a head pin with two rondelles and a niobium coil, and put the balls on eye pins with two rondelles and a niobium coil. Attach the disk pin to the ball pin and then attach it to the ear wire, which has been embellished with a niobium coil. (See above, right.)

STEP NINETEEN   Using the materials listed, string bracelet beads onto the tiger tail, alternating FIMO beads between two rondelles and a niobium coil. (See above, right.) Attach the split ring and clasp to the ends with crimp beads. See technique on page 11.

STEP TWENTY   Using the materials listed for the necklace, string all the beads onto the tiger tail. It is easiest to start in the center and work your way to the ends.

STEP TWENTY-ONE   Put the seed bead on the tiger tail. Fold the tiger tail in half and add a large round red

Close-up of necklace and earring beads.

Marbled Bracelet layout.

bead, a small blue coil, a green rondelle, the small FIMO disk bead, a pink rondelle, a small purple coil, a blue rondelle and the large disk bead, then split the tiger tail apart and add a large turquoise coil to each side. Continue stringing the beads on the tiger tail, making the sides symmetrical as you go. Finish by attaching a split ring to one side and the clasp to the other side using crimp beads.

MATERIALS

A variety of pieces of FIMO equal to
2 blocks

For the Earrings

2   blank sterling ear wires
4   sterling eye pins
4   sterling head pins
2 each—³/₁₆″ anodized niobium coils
     in navy, green and fuschia
     (niobium coils are a hard metal
     that has been colored using an
     electric charge.)
2 each—6mm rondelles in medium
     blue, red, pink and green

For the Bracelet

2 each—½″ anodized niobium coils
     in navy, green and purple
1 each—³/₁₆″ anodized niobium coils
     in navy, green and purple
2 each—6mm rondelles in green,
     yellow, lavender, red, cobalt,
     pink and aqua
1   sterling clasp
1   6mm split ring
12″ tiger tail
2   crimp beads

For the Necklace

½″ anodized niobium coils: 10 navy;
     8 purple; 8 fuschia; 2 aqua
1 each—³/₁₆″ anodized niobium coils
     in navy and purple
5   10mm red round beads
1   seed bead
1   6mm pink rondelle
3   6mm green rondelles
7   6mm cobalt rondelles
10 6mm aqua rondelles
3   6mm round red beads
4 each—6mm round beads in green
     and cobalt
4   8mm round cobalt beads
4   6mm green cylinder beads
2   4mm round aqua beads
2   8mm sterling split rings
1   sterling spring ring clasp
2   sterling crimp beads
40″ tiger tail

TOOLS

Knife
T-pins
No. 0 knitting needle
Needle-nose pliers
Round-nose pliers

*Marbled Bead Necklace, Earrings &
Bracelet embellished with anodized
niobium coils and glass beads.*

Spiral Cane Made of FIMO Leftovers

STEP ONE Separately knead the plain colors of FIMO in the food processor in the following order: Lilac, Light Turquoise, Red, Black. With a dry rag, clean the processor after each color. When the colors are removed from the processor, roll them each into a ball and set aside.

STEP TWO Throw all your scraps into the food processor and turn it on. Run the processor until beads form that are approximately $1/16''$ in diameter. Carefully remove them from the processor.

STEP THREE Gently roll the processed FIMO scraps into a ball and begin to flatten it out into a rectangle that is three to four times longer than it is wide. Keep the corners as square as possible.

STEP FOUR Roll out $1/4$ block of the Black until it will fit in the pasta machine on the No. 1 setting. Continue to put it through the machine to No. 4 and make sure it is large enough to cover the rectangle. If you are doing this by

Laying slices on top of a Black slab for the barrette.

hand, keep rolling it out until it is approximately $1/64''$ thick.

STEP FIVE Lay the black sheet on top of the rectangle and push out the air bubbles. Flip the clay over and trim the edges.

STEP SIX Follow the directions for creating a spiral cane with stripes, page 101. Use the Turquoise, Red and Lilac for the stripes.

STEP SEVEN Roll the cane down so there are sections in the following diameters: $1/2''$, $3/4''$, $1''$ and $1 1/4''$.

STEP EIGHT For the earring beads, take $1/4$ block of Black and divide it in half. Roll the clay into balls and apply slices of the cane on the surface. Blend in the slices by rolling the clay gently in your hands. Gently shape the balls into cylinders, put the beads on a T-pin and onto a baking sheet.

STEP NINE For the pin, take a $1/4$ block of Black and roll it into a ball, apply slices and blend them in. Gently flatten the clay into a disk slightly less than $1/4''$ thick. Set the disk flat on baking sheet.

STEP TEN For the barrette, use the last $1/4$ block of Black and roll it

out into a rectangle no less than $1/8''$ thick, $1 1/4''$ wide and $3 3/4''$ long. Lay out a variety of slices on the top (see second photo) and gently roll the slices into the Black with the cylinder. Trim to $1'' \times 3 1/2''$. Place the clay on a barrette clip, put the barrette on a baking sheet and cure all pieces in the oven.

STEP ELEVEN Attach the pin back and the barrette clip with cyano-acrylate glue.

STEP TWELVE For the earrings, put a head pin through each cylinder, add a purple bead and form an eye loop.

STEP THIRTEEN On a long ear wire, alternate three red and two turquoise beads. Form an eye loop and attach it to the FIMO cylinder bead.

Note: *When using the pasta machine with FIMO you need to roll the clay out first until it is fairly close to the size of the No. 1, opening. Otherwise, the FIMO will have stress lines in it when rolled through.*

FIMO scraps chopped up in the food processor.

MATERIALS

Any leftover FIMO

¼ block each of the following FIMO colors:

    #2 Red

    #60 Lilac

    #32 Light Turquoise

1   block of #9 Black

2   head pins

2   long French ear wires

1   1″ pin back

1   3″ barrette clip

6   6mm red glass beads

4   4mm turquoise glass beads

2   4mm purple glass beads

Cyanoacrylate glue

TOOLS

Old food processor with the cutting blade

Knife

Nonporous cylinder for rolling

OPTIONAL

Pasta machine

Spiral Cane Made of FIMO Leftovers.

Polka-Dot FIMO Cane

MATERIALS

1 block each of the following FIMO colors:
#0 White
#91 Anthracite
#8 Gray
⅛ to ¼ block of each of the following FIMO colors:
#39 Mint
#5 Green
#4 Orange
#32 Light Turquoise
#60 Lilac
#20 Pink
#15 Golden Yellow
#6 Violet
#2 Red
15 sterling silver head pins
5 sterling silver eye pins
2 sterling silver ear wires
2 sterling silver split rings
1 sterling silver spring ring clasp
24″ strong sterling silver link chain
A variety of bright glass beads—round and rondelles
Some large interesting glass beads from a bead store or directly from an artist.

TOOLS

T-pins
Knife
Round-nose pliers
Needle-nose pliers
Wire cutters

OPTIONAL

Pasta machine

Note: *You will have extra cane left over from this project to make more things.*

All the colors laid out, ready to form a cane.

STEP ONE Knead all the FIMO.

STEP TWO Roll all of the small pieces into ⅛″ to ¼″ diameter logs approximately 2½″ long. (See above.) Make two each of Lilac, Red, Green, Violet and Light Turquoise, and one each of the rest. Set extra pieces aside.

STEP THREE Roll out the Gray into a long rectangle 2½″ wide and slightly less than ¹⁄₁₆″ thick (a pasta machine works well for this).

STEP FOUR Wrap each log with Gray, and trim it.

STEP FIVE Lay the covered logs—touching—side by side, and place thin logs of Gray in the crevices. Pat the Gray logs in, flip the whole thing over, and repeat on the other side.

STEP SIX Make sure the pieces are fairly well attached to each other and roll them into a spiral. Once it is together, roll it until it is smooth. (See next page, top left.) Trim the ends.

STEP SEVEN Make black and white stripes (see Project 36 on page 101) and apply these to the outside of the Gray polka dot cane.

STEP EIGHT Roll out the cane to various diameters—1½″, 1¼″, 1″, ¾″, ½″, ⅜″ and ¼″.

STEP NINE Make thirteen beads for the necklace in a variety of shapes and sizes. Consider one large bead for the center. Use some of the leftover solid colors as the base of the necklace beads on which to apply small slices of cane. Put beads on T-pins and onto the baking rack.

The colored logs wrapped in Gray with thin filler lines.

Polka dots rolled into the Gray before adding the stripes.

STEP TEN For the earrings, cut two ¾″ disks ¼″ thick and one 1½″ in diameter. Cut the 1½″ disk in half. Put all the pieces on T-pins.

STEP ELEVEN Bake all the beads.

STEP TWELVE For the earrings, use an eye pin for the disks. Embellish with glass beads and attach to ear wires. Use head pins for the half circles (flat edge down). Embellish with glass beads and attach to the disks.

Complete polka-dot cane in pieces of various sizes.

STEP THIRTEEN Embellish the necklace beads with glass beads on head pins or eye pins (depending on how you are stacking the beads). Attach these to the silver chain at equal intervals approximately 1¼″ to 1½″ apart.

STEP FOURTEEN Attach a split ring to each end of the chain and a spring ring clasp to one end.

Polka-dot beads ready to be made into a necklace and earrings.

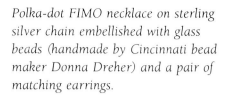

Polka-dot FIMO necklace on sterling silver chain embellished with glass beads (handmade by Cincinnati bead maker Donna Dreher) and a pair of matching earrings.

Black & White FIMO Face Cane

MATERIALS

2 blocks FIMO #0 White
½ block FIMO #9 Black
Tiger tail
2   sterling silver ear wires
2   sterling silver eye pins
6   sterling silver head pins
2   1″ pin backs
2   sterling silver crimp beads
1   sterling silver split ring
1   sterling silver spring ring clasp
Colorful glass beads

TOOLS

Knife
Needle-nose pliers
Round-nose pliers
T-pins

STEP ONE   Knead the FIMO.

STEP TWO   Make the eyes first (They should be 1″ square and approximately ¾″ thick) by placing the shapes together as plotted out in the pattern shown in the photo below, left.

STEP THREE   Reduce the eye to ½″ square by gently squeezing and pulling the sides.

STEP FOUR   Cut the eye cane in half, flip one piece over and set it in place.

STEP FIVE   Make a spiral for the hair, but don't roll it up completely— leave a tail. (See Steps One through Five on page 101.) Make it as thick as the eyes.

STEP SIX   Form the nose and mouth out of Black, making them the same thickness as the eyes and hair.

STEP SEVEN   Build up the face starting with the eyes and filling in with White shapes as shown in the pattern in the second photo.

STEP EIGHT   Once all the shapes are in place, gently begin reducing the cane by squeezing and pulling from the sides. Keep reforming the outside shape and make sure not to twist. Reduce until the face is 1⅜″ high and 1″ wide.

STEP NINE   Cut four face slices ¼″ thick.

STEP TEN   Reduce the cane further

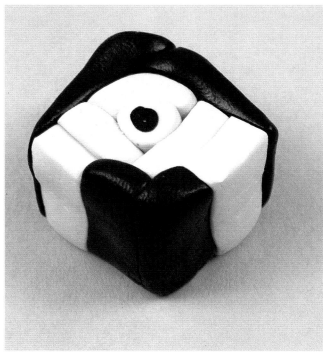

The eye parts put together.

The layered pieces forming the face. At this point, it is approximately 1½″ thick.

until the face is 1³⁄₁₆″ high and ³⁄₄″ wide.

STEP ELEVEN Cut seven slices approximately ³⁄₁₆″ thick.

STEP TWELVE With T-pins, pierce through two of the larger slices from the top of the head to the chin and set it on a baking rack.

STEP THIRTEEN Pierce the rest of the faces through where the ears would be. Set these on the baking rack and cure.

STEP FOURTEEN Use colorful glass beads to make the necklace and earrings. (See photo of the finished pieces, opposite.)

STEP FIFTEEN For the pins, run an eye pin through the head and make a loop on the other side. Make head pins with beads approximately 1″ long and attach these to eye loops on the face. It makes the faces look as though they have earrings on.

The first slices of the completed cane.
The face is 1³⁄₈″ high and 1″ wide.

Black and White FIMO Face Cane Earrings, Necklace & Pins embellished with colorful glass beads.

Gallery of Polymer Clay Jewelry

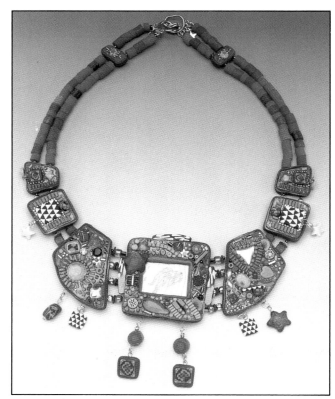

Jean Hornberger, Laurel, DE
No 1.
Polymer clay
8½" × 11"
©1994

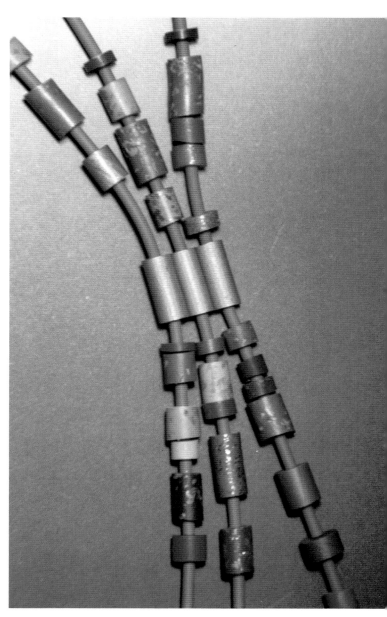

Lindly Haunani, Bethesda, MD
Three Way Split
Polymer clay, rubber cord, glitter, horn
beads
32"
©1994

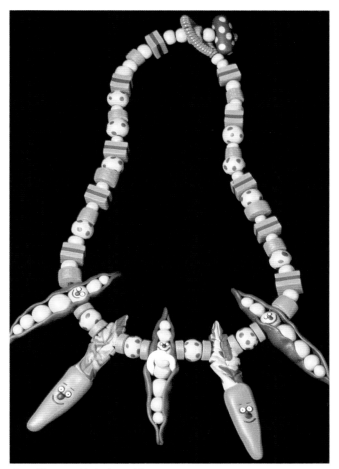

Amy Zinman, Hoboken, NJ
Peas & Carrots Necklace
Polymer clay
20"
©1991

Mary Lyon, Los Angeles, CA
Faux Ivory
Polymer clay
18"
©1994

Klew Expressions, Tehachapi, CA
Mardi Gras Queen Brooch
FIMO, PROMAT, gold leafing, metallic
powders, (ten separate canes)
4" × 2"
©1995

RESOURCES

ELECTRONIC & HARDWARE SURPLUS

Mendelson Electronic Co., Inc.
340 E. 1st St.
Dayton, OH 45402
1-513-461-3525
100,000-ft. retail store filled with wonderful items.
Hours: Monday - Saturday 8:30 A.M.- 5:00 P.M.

JEWELRY TOOLS AND FINDINGS

TSI
101 Nickerson Street
P.O. Box 9266
Seattle, WA 98109
206-282-3040
1-800-426-9984 outside WA
Free sales flyer.
Wholesale and retail mail order and store; carries tools, findings, beads and more.

Ball Group Corporation
　Rio Grande Albuquerque (Tools)
　4516 Anaheim Ave. NE
　Albuquerque, NM 87113-1668
　1-800-545-6566

　River Gems and Findings
　(Beads and Findings)
　6901 Washington NE
　Albuquerque, NM 87109-4490
　1-800-648-3499

$10/catalog; free with tax ID number; wholesale and retail suppliers.

Rings and Things
214 North Wall Ave. Suite 990
P.O. Box 450
Spokane, WA 99210-0450
1-800-366-2156
$5 catalog.
Production supplier of general jewelry supplies; mail order and store.

East West DyeCom, Inc.
P.O. Box 12294
Roanoke, VA 24024
703-362-1489
$5 catalog, refunded on the first order. Anodized aluminum products. Retail—discounts on quantity.

POLYMER CLAY SUPPLIERS

American Art Clay Co., Inc.
4717 W. 16th St.
Indianapolis, IN 46222
317-244-6871
Free catalog; FIMO, Friendly Clay and Friendly Plastic.

Dee's Delights
3150 Stateline Road
Cincinnati, OH 45052
513-353-3390
$3 for brochure; wholesale only; FIMO.

The Clay Factory
P.O. Box 1270
Escondido, CA 92025
619-741-3242
Free catalog; wholesale and retail. FIMO, Cernit, Sculpey III, Super Sculpey, PROMAT.

FURTHER INFO ON POLYMER CLAY

National Polymer Clay Guild
1350 Beverly Rd.
Suite 115-345
McLean, VA 22101
202-895-5212 (information number)
Annual membership $20, September 1 through August 31. Bimonthly newsletter: POLYinfoMER. There are chapters around the country.

The New Clay *by Nan Roche, © 1991, Flower Valley Press, Rockville, MD. (And look for* The New Clay 2 *by Nan Roche, Flower Valley Press, Rockville, MD.)*

Creative Clay Jewelry *by Leslie Dierks, ©1994, Lark Books, Asheville, NC.*

I N D E X

A

Anodized aluminum pin and earrings, 40-41
Anodized niobium coils, 9
Awls, 8

B

Barrel clasps, 9
Barrette clips, 9
Barrettes
    FIMO, 101-103
Beads
    poly-fil bead necklace and earrings, 60-61
    recycled plastic disks with dangling beads, 80-81
    tube necklace and bracelet with seed beads, 86-87
Black and white FIMO face cane, 117-119
Black sheet rubber feathered necklace and earrings, 94-95
Bolos
    "Tone/Volume Bolos," 43
Bracelets, 42
    marbled bead bracelet, 110-111
    rubber O-ring gasket bracelet, 90-91
    tube bracelets with seed beads, 86-87
Brass gasket earrings, 34-35
Button covers, 9
Buttons
    elastic button bracelet, 20-21
    Sculpey III striped spiral buttons, 104-105
    squiggly button barrettes, 18-19
    stacked button pins, 16-17

C

Cable tie earrings and pins, 30-31
Canes
    polka-dot FIMO cane, 114-116
    spiral cane from FIMO leftovers, 112-113
Cermit, 99
Clasps, barrel, 9
Clays, polymer— see Polymer clays.
Clips, barrette, 9
Collage fabric pins, 54-55
Collage paper pins, 46-47
Constructed wood pin, 64-65
Cords
    placing crimps at end of, 12
Crimp beads, 9

finishing tiger tail with, 11
Crimps, 9
    cord, placing at end of, 12
Curing process, polymer clays, 99
Cut-out plastic laminate earrings and pin, 78-79
Cutting
    jeweler's saw, 13

D

Dehner, Sheila
    "Button Necklace #7," 42
Dennis, Dianne
    "Needlepoint Pin," 70
Dreher, Donna, 116
Dremel Moto-tool, 8
    drilling holes, 12
Dyed turned wood earrings and pin, 66-67

E

Ear loops, 9
Ear nuts, 9
Earring posts, 9
Earrings
    anodized aluminum earrings, 40-41
    black and white FIMO face cane earrings, 119
    black sheet rubber feathered earrings, 94-95
    brass gasket earrings, 34-35
    cable tie earrings, 30-31
    cut-out plastic laminate earrings, 78-79
    dyed turned wood earrings, 66-67
    electrically connected earrings, 22-23
    fabric covered gasket earrings, 32-33
    faucet strainer earrings, 38-39
    FIMO, 101-103
    FIMO face earrings, 108-109
    folded gift paper pin, 48-49
    folded window screen, 36-37
    Friendly Plastic earrings, 82-85
    Fun Foam earrings, 88-89
    layered tissue paper earrings, 52-53
    marbled bead earrings, 110-111
    "Paper Earrings," 71
    plastic confetti earrings, 74-75
    plastic grid earrings, 76-77
    polka-dot FIMO earrings, 116
    poly-fil bead earrings, 60-61
    resistor earrings, 24-25
    rolled ribbon earrings, 56-57
    Sculpey III herringbone pattern coiled

earrings, 106-107
    stacked colorful rubber tubing earrings, 92-93
    wood hand earrings, 68-69
    Woodsie earrings, 62-63
Elastic button bracelet, 20-21
Electrical wire connectors
    electrically connected earrings, 22-23
Embellished pillow pins, 58-59
Eye loops on head pins, 11
Eye pins, 9

F

Fabric
    embellished pillow pins, 58-59
    fabric collage pins, 54-55
    "Needlepoint Pin," 70
    poly-fil bead necklace and earrings, 60-61
    rolled ribbon earrings and pin, 56-57
    "Way Out," 70
Fabric covered gasket pin, 32-33
Fancy resistor and bead necklace, 28-29
Faucet strainer earrings and necklace, 38-39
Fiber, 45-72
    gallery, 70-71
FIMO, 99
    barrette, 101-103
    black and white FIMO face cane, 117-119
    earrings, 101-103
    face pins and earrings, 108-109
    kneading, 100
    marbled bead necklace, earrings, and bracelet, 110-111
    necklace, 101-103
    pin, 101-103
    polka-dot FIMO cane, 114-116
    polka-dot FIMO necklace and earrings, 116
    preparing, 100
    spiral cane from FIMO leftovers, 112-113
Findings—see also specific finding.
Folded gift paper pin and earrings, 48-49
Folded window screen earrings and pin, 36-37
Found objects, 15-44—see also specific found object.
French ear wires, 9
Friendly plastic pins and earrings, 82-85

Fun foam earrings and pin, 88-89

G

Gallery, 42-43, 70-71, 96-97, 120-121
Gaskets
    brass gasket earrings, 34-35
    fabric covered gasket pin and earrings, 32-33
    rubber O-ring gasket bracelet, 90-91
Glue guns, 8
    using, 10
Gluing pin backs, 10
Grape, Carol
    "Braided Squiggle Pin," 96
    "42-50 Necklace," 97
    "Red Finger Necklace," 96
    "X Spot Pin," 97

H

Hand pin and earrings, wood, 68-69
Hardware charm necklace, 26-27
Harper, Cam
    "Cosmic Cartographer," 42
Harris, Renee
    "Way Out," 70
Haunani, Lindly
    "Three Way Split," 120
Head pins, 9
    eye loops on, forming, 11
Herringbone pattern pins and coiled
    earrings, Sculpey III, 106-107
Hornberger, Jean
    "No. 1," 120

I

Introduction, 7

J

Jenkins, Ann
    "Bracelet," 42
Jeweler's saw, 8
    cutting, 13
Jewelry findings, 8-14— see also specific
    finding.
Jump rings, 9
    opening and closing, 10

K

Keith, Bill
    "Bracelet," 42
Klew Expressions
    "Mardi Gras Queen Brooch," 121
Knives, utility, 8

L

Layered tissue paper earrings and pin, 52-53
Lobster claw clasps, 9
Lyon, Mary
    "Faux Ivory," 121

M

Marbled bead necklace, earrings, and
    bracelet, 110-111
Metal ear wires, 9
Meyerowitz, Patricia
    "Pendant and Chain," 43
Mixing polymer clays, 99

N

Naylor, Susan
    "Stripes and Grids," 71
Necklace chain, 9
Necklaces
    black and white FIMO face cane neck-
      lace, 119
    black sheet rubber feathered necklace, 94-95
    "Button Necklace #7," 42
    fancy resistor and bead necklace, 28-29
    faucet strainer necklaces, 38-39
    FIMO, 101-103
    "42-50 Necklace," 97
    hardware charm necklace, 26-27
    marbled bead necklace, 110-111
    plastic grid necklace, 76-77
    polka-dot FIMO necklace, 116
    poly-fil bead necklace, 60-61
    "Red Finger Necklace," 96
    stacked colorful rubber tubing necklace, 92-93
    tube necklace with seed beads, 86-87
Needle-nose pliers, 8

O

O-ring gasket bracelet, rubber, 90-91

P

Paper, 45-72
    collage paper pins, 46-47
    folded gift paper pin and earrings, 48-49
    gallery, 70-71
    layered tissue paper earrings and pin, 52-53
    "Paper Earrings," 71
    sponge-painted paper hearts, 50-51
    "Stripes and Grids," 71
Pendants
    "Pendant and Chain," 43
Phone wire
    electrically connected earrings, 22-23
    squiggly button barrettes, 18-19
Pin backs, 9
    gluing, 10
Pins
    anodized aluminum pin, 40-41
    black and white FIMO face cane pins, 119
    "Braided Squiggle Pin," 96
    cable tie pins, 30-31
    collage paper pins, 46-47
    constructed wood pin, 64-65
    cut-out plastic laminate pins, 78-79
    dyed turned wood pin, 66-67
    embellished pillow pins, 58-59
    fabric collage pins, 54-55
    fabric covered gasket pin, 32-33
    FIMO, 101-103
    FIMO face pins, 108-109
    folded gift paper pin, 48-49
    folded window screen pin, 36-37
    Friendly Plastic pins, 82-85
    Fun Foam pins, 88-89
    layered tissue paper pin, 52-53
    "Needlepoint Pin," 70
    plastic confetti pins, 74-75
    rolled ribbon pins, 56-57
    Sculpey III herringbone pattern pins, 106-107
    wood hand pin, 68-69

Woodsie pins, 62-63
"X Spot Pin," 97
Plastic, 72-97
    confetti earrings and pins, 74-75
    cut-out plastic laminate earrings and pin,
        78-79
    Friendly Plastic pins and earrings, 82-85
    Fun Foam earrings and pin, 88-89
    gallery, 96-97
    grid necklace and earrings, 76-77
    recycled plastic disks with dangling
        beads, 80-81
    tube necklace and bracelet with seed
        beads, 86-87
Pliers
    needle-nose, 8
    round-nose, 8
Polka-dot FIMO cane, 114-116
Poly-fil bead necklace and earrings, 60-61
Polymer clays, 98-121
    barrette, FIMO, 101-103
    black and white FIMO face cane,
        117-119
    Cermit, 99
    curing process, 99
    earrings, FIMO, 101-103
    face pins and earrings, FIMO, 108-109
    "Faux Ivory," 121
    FIMO, 99-103— see also FIMO.
    gallery, 120-121
    herringbone pattern pins and coiled ear-
        rings, sculpey III, 106-107
    kneading FIMO, 100
    marbled bead necklace, earrings, and
        bracelet, 110-111
    "Mardi Gras Queen Brooch," 121
    mixing, 99
    necklace, FIMO, 101-103
    "No 1," 120
    "Peas & Carrots Necklace," 121
    pin, FIMO, 101-103
    polka-dot FIMO cane, 114-116
    preparing FIMO, 100
    safety tips, 100
    Sculpey III, 99, 104-107

    spiral cane from FIMO leftovers,
        112-113
    striped spiral buttons, Sculpey III,
        104-107
    "Three Way Split," 120

R
Recycled plastic disks with dangling beads,
    80-81
Resistors
    fancy resistor and bead necklace, 28-29
    resistor earrings, 24-25
Resources, 122
Rolled ribbon earrings and pin, 56-57
Ross, Karl
    "Timely Revivals," 43
Round-nose pliers, 8
Rubber, 72-97
    black sheet rubber feathered necklace
        and earrings, 94-95
    fun foam earrings and pin, 88-89
    gallery, 96-97
    O-ring gasket bracelet, 90-91
    stacked colorful rubber tubing necklace
        and earrings, 92-93

S
Safety tips, polymer clays, 100
Salzer, Miriam
    "Tone/Volume Bolos," 43
Saws, jeweler's, 8
Screw eyes without threads, 9
Sculpey III, 99, 104-107
    herringbone pattern pins and coiled ear-
        rings, 106-107
    striped spiral buttons, 104-105
Spiral cane from FIMO leftovers, 112-113
Split rings, 9
Sponge-painted paper hearts, 50-51
Spring ring clasps, 9
Squiggly button barrettes, 18-19
Stacked button pins, 16-17
Stacked colorful rubber tubing necklace
    and earrings, 92-93
Striped spiral buttons, Sculpey III, 104-105

T
Tait, Elizabeth
    "Paper Earrings," 71
Techniques, 8-14—see also specific tech-
    nique.
Thompson, Nancy Kunkle
    "Brooch," 96
Tiger tail, 9
    finishing with crimp beads, 11
Tools, 8-14—see also specific tool.
T-pins, 8
Tube necklace and bracelet with seed
    beads, plastic, 86-87

U
Utility knives, 8

W
Window screen
    folded window screen earrings and pin,
        36-37
Wire cutters, 8
Wires
    French ear wires, 9
    holding findings in place, 13
    metal ear wires, 9
    phone wire, 18-19, 22-23
Wood, 45-72
    constructed wood pin, 64-65
    dyed turned wood earrings and pin,
        66-67
    gallery, 70-71
    hand pin and earrings, 68-69
    woodsie earrings and pin, 62-63
Woodsie earrings and pin, 62-63

Z
Zinman, Amy
    "Peas & Carrots Necklace," 121

More Great Books for Creating Beautiful Crafts

Creative Wall Decorating—Turn your walls—and your rooms—into masterpieces with this idea-filled book. You'll find exciting examples of innovative techniques including stenciling, sponge painting, rubber stamping and more. Plus, brilliant color photos and easy-to-follow instructions make your decorating as easy as 1-2-3. *#70317/$16.99/128 pages/ 250 + color illus./paperback*

How to Start Making Money with Your Crafts—Launch a rewarding crafts business with this guide that starts with the basics—from creating marketable products to setting the right prices—and explores all the exciting possibilities. End-of-chapter quizzes, worksheets, ideas and lessons learned by successful crafters are included to increase your learning curve. *#70302/$18.99/176 pages/35 b&w illus.*

Creative Paint Finishes for Furniture—Revive your furniture with fresh color and design! Inexpensive, easy and fun painting techniques are at your fingertips, along with step-by-step directions and a photo gallery of imaginative applications for faux finishing, staining, stenciling, mosaic, découpage and many other techniques. *#30748/$27.99/144 pages/ 236 color, 7 b&w illus.*

Dried Flowers: Colors for Every Room in the House—Create exquisite arrangements to match any room or color scheme! With this versatile and easy-to-use reference, you'll discover the full range of available flower types, as well as step-by-step projects and a gallery of arrangements to inspire your work! *#30701/$27.99/144 pages/4-color throughout*

The Crafts Supply Sourcebook—Turn here to find the materials you need—from specialty tools and the hardest-to-find accessories, to clays, doll parts, patterns, quilting machines and hundreds of other items! Listings organized by area of interest make it quick and easy! *#70253/$16.99/288 pages/25 b&w illus./ paperback*

Stencil Source Book 2—Add color and excitement to fabrics, furniture, walls and more with over 200 original motifs that can be used again and again! Idea-packed chapters will help you create dramatic color schemes and themes to enhance your home in hundreds of ways. *#30730/$22.99/144 pages/300 illus.*

The Complete Book of Silk Painting—Create fabulous fabric art—everything from clothing to pillows to wall hangings. You'll learn every aspect of silk painting in this step-by-step guide, including setting up a workspace, necessary materials and fabrics and specific silk painting techniques. *#30362/$26.99/128 pages/color throughout*

Fabric Sculpture: The Step-By-Step Guide & Showcase—Discover how to transform fabrics into 3-dimensional images. Seven professional fabric sculptors demonstrate projects that illustrate their unique approaches and methods for creating images from fabric. The techniques—covered in easy, step-by-step illustration and instruction—include quilting, thread work, applique and soft sculpture. *#30687/$29.99/160 pages/ 300 + color illus.*

Decorative Wreaths & Garlands—Discover stylish, yet simple-to-make wreaths and garlands. These 20 original designs use fabrics and fresh and dried flowers to add color and personality to any room, and charm to special occasions. Clear instructions are accompanied by step-by-step photographs to ensure that you create a perfect display every time. *#30696/$19.99/96 pages/175 color illus./ paperback*

The Complete Flower Arranging Book—An attractive, up-to-date guide to creating more than 100 beautiful arrangements with fresh and dried flowers, illustrated with step-by-step demonstrations. *#30405/$24.95/192 pages/300 + color illus.*

The Complete Flower Craft Book—Discover techniques for drying fresh flowers and seedheads, creating arrangements to suit all seasons and occasions, making silk flowers, potpourri, bath oil and more! This guide is packed with photographs, tips and step-by-step instructions to give you a bouquet of ideas and inspiration! *#30589/$24.95/144 pages/ 275 color illus.*

Jewelry & Accessories: Beautiful Designs to Make and Wear—Discover how to make unique jewelry out of papier maché, wood, leather, cloth and metals. You'll learn how to create: a hand-painted wooden brooch, a silk-painted hair slide, a paper and copper necklace and much more! Fully illustrated with step-by-step

instructions. *#30680/$17.99/128 pages/ 150 color illus./paperback*

The Art of Painting Animals on Rocks—Discover how a dash of paint can turn humble stones into charming "pet rocks." This hands-on, easy-to-follow book offers a menagerie of fun—and potentially profitable—stone animal projects. Eleven examples, complete with material list, photos of the finished piece and patterns will help you create a forest of fawns, rabbits, foxes and other adorable critters. *#30606/$21.99/144 pages/250 color illus./paperback*

Decorative Boxes To Create, Give and Keep—Craft beautiful boxes using techniques including embroidery, stenciling, lacquering, gilding, shellwork, decoupage and many others. Step-by-step instructions and photographs detail every project. *#30638/$15.95/128 pages/color throughout/paperback*

Elegant Ribboncraft—Over 40 ideas for exquisite ribbon-craft—hand-tied bows, floral garlands, ribbon embroidery and more. Various techniques are employed—including folding, pleating, plaiting, weaving, embroidery, patchwork, quilting, applique and decoupage. All projects are complete with step-by-step instructions and photographs. *#30697/$16.99/ 128 pages/130 + color illus.*

Paint Craft—Discover great ideas for enhancing your home, wardrobe and personal items. You'll see how to master the basics of mixing and planning colors, how to print with screen and linoleum to create your own stationery, how to enhance old glassware and pottery pieces with unique patterns and motifs and much more! *#30678/$16.99/144 pages/200 color illus./paperback*

Nature Craft—Dozens of step-by-step nature craft projects to create, including dried flower garlands, baskets, corn dollies, potpourri and more. Bring the outdoors inside with these wonderful projects crafted with readily available natural materials. *#30531/$14.95/144 pages/200 color illus./paperback*

Paper Craft—Dozens of step-by-step paper craft projects to make, including greeting cards, boxes and desk sets, jewelry and pleated paper blinds. If you have ever worked with or wanted to work with paper you'll enjoy these attractive, fun-to-make projects. *#30530/$16.95/144 pages/ 200 color illus./paperback*

Everything You Ever Wanted to Know About Fabric Painting—Discover how to create beautiful fabrics! You'll learn how to set up work space, choose materials, plus the ins and outs of tie-dye, screen printing, woodgraining, marbling, cyanotype and more! #30625/$21.99/128 pages/color throughout/paperback

Holiday Fun with Dian Thomas—Discover how to turn mere holiday observances into opportunities to exercise imagination and turn the festivity all the way up. You'll find suggestions for a memorable New Year's celebration, silly April Fool's Day pranks, recipes and ideas for a Labor Day family get-together, creative Christmas giving and much more! #70300/$19.99/144 pages/150 color illus./paperback

The Teddy Bear Sourcebook: For Collectors and Crafters—Discover the most complete treasury of bear information stuffed between covers. You'll turn here whenever you need to find sellers of bear making supplies, major manufacturers of teddy bears, teddy bear shows, auctions and contests, museums that house teddy bear collections and much more. #70294/$18.99/356 pages/202 illus./paperback

Master Strokes—Master the techniques of decorative painting with this comprehensive guide! Learn to use decorative paint finishes on everything from small objects and furniture to walls and floors, including dozens of step-by-step demonstrations and numerous techniques. #30347/$29.99/160 pages/400 color illus.

Master Works: How to Use Paint Finishes to Transform Your Surroundings— Discover how to use creative paint finishes to enhance and excite the "total look" of your home. This step-by-step guide contains dozens of exciting ideas on fresco, marbling, paneling and other simple paint techniques for bringing new life to any space. Plus, you'll also find innovative uses for fabrics, screens and blinds. #30626/$29.95/176 pages/150 color illus.

Creative Paint Finishes for the Home—A complete, full-color step-by-step guide to decorating floors, walls and furniture—including how to use the tools, master the techniques and develop ideas. #30426/$27.99/144 pages/212 color illus.

Stencil Source Book—Transform a room from plain to remarkable. This guide combines inspiration with practical information—and more than 180 original designs you can turn into stencils. #30595/$22.95/144 pages/150 color illus.

Painting Murals—Learn through eight step-by-step projects how to choose a subject for a mural, select colors that will create the desired effects and transfer the design to the final surface. #30081/$29.99/168 pages/125 color illus.

Create Your Own Greeting Cards and Gift Wrap with Priscilla Hauser—You'll see sponge prints, eraser prints, cellophane scrunching, marbleizing, paper making and dozens of other techniques you can use to make unique greetings for all your loved ones. #30621/$24.99/128 pages/230 color illus.

How to Airbrush T-Shirts and Other Clothing—Make a statement—or a living—by painting clothing. You'll learn how to create popular subjects and lettering styles, design stencils—plus, how to price and sell your work! #30614/$24.99/128 pages/200+ color, 15 b&w illus./paperback

Airbrush Action 2—Jump-start your creativity with over 400 fresh, exciting images from top airbrush artists. You'll find works in acrylic, gouache and watercolor in full color with credits. #30662/$29.95/192 pages/450+ color illus./paperback

Getting Started in Airbrush—A step-by-step guide to all the basic-level airbrush techniques used to create a wide variety of effects when doing commercial illustration or airbrushing a T-shirt. Key airbrushing techniques are shown and described in action. #30514/$22.99/128 pages/200 color, 30 b&w illus./paperback

Basic Airbrush Painting Techniques—Beginning airbrush artists—find everything you need to know, from choosing the right materials to creating dazzling airbrush effects. #30570/$19.95/128 pages/230 color illus./paperback

Basic Drawing Techniques—Seven outstanding artists, including Bert Dodson, Charles Sovek and Frank Webb, share their drawing techniques and teach you how to use popular drawing mediums. #30332/$16.99/128 pages/128 b&w illus./paperback

First Steps Series: Sketching and Drawing—You'll find great advice for beginning artists on how to draw believable trees, fruit, flowers, skies, water and more. Simple step-by-step directions and demonstrations show you how to put it all together into a finished product. Also included are easy and useful tips for blending, shading, perspective and other techniques to help you create realistic drawings. #30719/$18.99/128 pages/121 illus./paperback

First Steps Series: Painting Watercolors—Discover everything you need to begin painting! Exercises will help you loosen up and learn the ins and outs of putting paint on paper. Step-by-step directions and a dozen demonstrations will show you how paintings come together, from initial sketch to final brushstroke. #30724/$18.99/128 pages/150 color and b&w illus./paperback

Perspective Without Pain—A hands-on guide featuring simple language and exercises to help you conquer your fears about perspective in drawing. #30386/$19.99/144 pages/185 color illus./paperback